mindfulness FIRST

A **NINE-WEEK LEADERSHIP PLAN**
FOR SUPPORTING YOURSELF AND YOUR SCHOOL

Jeanie M. Iberlin

Foreword by Robert J. Marzano

MARZANO
Resources

555 North Morton Street
Bloomington, IN 47404
888.849.0851
FAX: 866.801.1447

email: info@MarzanoResources.com
MarzanoResources.com

Visit **MarzanoResources.com/reproducibles** to download the free reproducibles in this book.

Printed in the United States of America

Library of Congress Cataloging-in-Publication Data

Names: Iberlin, Jeanie M., author.

Title: Mindfulness first : a nine-week leadership plan for supporting
    yourself and your school / Jeanie M. Iberlin.

Description: Bloomington, IN : Marzano Resources, 2023. | Includes
    bibliographical references and index.

Identifiers: LCCN 2022038330 (print) | LCCN 2022038331 (ebook) | ISBN
    9781943360765 (paperback) | ISBN 9781943360772 (ebook)

Subjects: LCSH: Educational leadership--Psychological aspects. |
    Mindfulness (Psychology) | Teacher-administrator relationships. |
    Mindfulness (Psychology)--Research. | Teachers--Job stress--Prevention.

Classification: LCC LB2806 .I24 2023 (print) | LCC LB2806 (ebook) | DDC
    371.2--dc23/eng/20220919

LC record available at https://lccn.loc.gov/2022038330

LC ebook record available at https://lccn.loc.gov/2022038331

Production Team
President and Publisher: Douglas M. Rife
Associate Publisher: Sarah Payne-Mills
Managing Production Editor: Kendra Slayton
Editorial Director: Todd Brakke
Art Director: Rian Anderson
Copy Chief: Jessi Finn
Production Editor: Alissa Voss
Content Development Specialist: Amy Rubenstein
Copy Editor: Evie Madsen
Proofreader: Mark Hain
Text and Cover Designer: Fabiana Cochran
Associate Editor: Sarah Ludwig
Editorial Assistants: Charlotte Jones and Elijah Oates

For nearly three decades, I have been an avid practitioner of mindfulness. It has helped me find peace and centeredness as an educator, a school and district leader, a wife, and a parent. Throughout those years, my daughter, Danielle Barent Breen, has been my mindfulness sidekick. When she was just two years old, she would often sit on my lap during my mindful meditations. She knew it was quiet time, so she, for the most part, would sit still while occasionally reaching up to pat my face. We would go on mindful nature walks together in the Big Horn Mountains near Buffalo, Wyoming, taking time to notice the sound of the creek or the crunch of the crisp fall leaves beneath our feet. We would enjoy mindful eating with agreed-on rules, such as no cell phones at the table during meals. We practiced mindful listening, helping one another through difficult times by being fully present and hearing what the other had to say. Danielle serves as a structural firefighter in Denver, Colorado. Her mindfulness practice has aided her in facing very trying situations as a first responder. We are both aware that mindfulness is not a cure-all, and yet we can both attest to the peace and sense of aliveness it has brought to our lives. It is with great love that I dedicate this book to my daughter, Danielle.

—Jeanie M. Iberlin

Table of Contents

Acknowledgments

I have immense gratitude for the Solution Tree and Marzano Resources staffs, especially my editor, Alissa Voss. Her insight added so much to my work.

Thank you to Dr. Robert J. Marzano for his thoughtful foreword.

I also extend gratitude to all school leaders for their dedication to students' and staff members' learning and well-being. Your career is not an easy one, but it is a very worthy one.

Solution Tree and Marzano Resources would like to thank the following reviewers:

Heather Bell-Williams
    Principal, Milltown
        Elementary School
    Anglophone South School District
    St. Stephen, New Brunswick, Canada

Chris Bennett
    Principal
    Burns Middle School
    Lawndale, North Carolina

Angie Bryan
    Principal
    Brown Elementary
    Reno, Nevada

Harold Freiter
    Principal
    Lockport School
    Lockport, Manitoba, Canada

Visit **MarzanoResources.com/reproducibles** to download the free reproducibles in this book.

About the Author

eanie M. Iberlin, EdD, has nearly forty years of experience in education. Before retiring, she served as associate superintendent of Johnson County School District in Wyoming, where she led administrators, instructional facilitators, teachers, and other staff members in the areas of curriculum, instruction, assessment, evaluation, and professional development.

Dr. Iberlin has been honored as Wyoming Assistant Superintendent of the Year for her leadership in the areas of assessment, curriculum, and instruction. She has served as a middle school principal and high school English teacher, and she has served on several state committees.

Dr. Iberlin earned an undergraduate degree from Chadron State College in Nebraska, a master's degree from the University of Wyoming, and a doctoral degree from Montana State University.

Foreword

By Robert J. Marzano

This new book by Jeanie M. Iberlin provides a unique perspective on leadership in that it begins with a focus on leaders recognizing they must work on the inner world of human thought if they are to maximize their effectiveness in the outer world of leadership. This is precisely the perspective articulated in *Managing the Inner World of Teaching: Emotions, Interpretations, and Actions* (Marzano & Marzano, 2015). A tacit premise underlying the suggestions in Iberlin's book is that the more aware leaders are of their thoughts and feelings, the more able they are to lead in a manner that is not only effective but also supportive of and nurturing to those who are being led. The term for such awareness is *mindfulness.*

Although the term *mindfulness* appears in many books, it is commonly not well defined or described. For Iberlin, it starts with an awareness of what one is thinking and feeling at any given point in time. This is not a natural state nor an easy one to achieve. It requires conscious effort exerted over time. Iberlin addresses a wide variety of techniques for achieving this state, all of which have the pleasant side effect of lowering one's stress level. This is noteworthy in and of itself. These techniques are not based on any set of spiritual principles or associated with any religious orientation; rather, Iberlin takes pains to cite the research and theory supporting the positive physiological effects of the techniques she provides. Many of them, like the *mindful pause*, can be executed in a brief interval of time. Here, leaders simply take a quick break from their daily routines and events to notice their thoughts and feelings. Powerful generalizations can arise from such moments, with perhaps the most powerful of these focused on the relationship between strong negative emotions and one's thinking at any point in time. Stated differently, when people experience strong negative emotions such as anger, fear, or anxiety, their thinking is severely skewed. They will likely come to conclusions they would not have reached in the absence of the strong negative emotions, and those conclusions can involve proposed negative behavior to the hypothesized cause of the anger, fear, or anxiety. In effect, reaching the state of equilibrium mindfulness generates can be a deterrent to reactive and potentially damaging behavior on the part of leaders—again, an outcome noteworthy in and of itself.

Once leaders start to cultivate the discipline of mindfulness, a number of actions become available to them that were previously not even within their consciousness. One of these is *mindful listening*. This goes well beyond *active listening*, which involves communicating to the speaker that the message has been received and understood. Mindful listening adds self-refection on the part of the listener, who takes note of thoughts and feelings about the speaker's message.

Perhaps, the most important message in Iberlin's discussion is the power of human intentions. She posits that human beings act in accordance with their intentions even when they are not overtly aware of those intentions. Tacit intentions commonly emanate from natural human tendencies for self-preservation and control. While these are understandable human dynamics, a case can be made that the most powerful position leaders can take is to ask themselves what their intended outcome is regarding their planned actions relative to the situation at hand and, if it manifests, how beneficial that outcome would be for all.

Mindfulness First is not your typical educational leadership book. Readers will find that it increases their effectiveness with their constituents and gives them enhanced efficacy and agency relative to their own lives.

Introduction

I found mindfulness—or, rather, mindfulness found me—when I was attending graduate school to earn a master's degree in educational leadership. At the time, I was working full-time as a high school English teacher and raising my two-year-old daughter and fourteen-year-old stepson alongside my husband (who was a teacher and a coach), while attending weekend classes in a town four hours away. Overwhelmed and needing to ground myself, I was invited to participate in a local mindful meditation course.

The first time I closed my eyes and focused on my in-breath and out-breath, I could feel my shoulders and jaw begin to relax. Tears of relief sprang from my eyes, and tension seeped from my body. Within minutes, my heart felt lighter. I was hooked! Mindful meditation became a part of my daily practice. Since 1991, despite my busy schedule, I have set my alarm early enough to allow myself to sit mindfully for fifteen to thirty minutes each morning. This practice has become an integral part of my daily routine, along with numerous other mindfulness practices, many of which I describe in this book.

When I became a middle school principal and, later, an associate superintendent, my mindfulness practice became central to my role as a leader. It was especially helpful when dealing with emotionally charged situations. By mindfully centering myself each morning and again directly before, during, and after intense conversations, I was able to de-escalate potentially hostile dialogues and behaviors. Further, I was able to stay centered or re-center quickly, allowing me to give my all to the next situation or task.

I recall one incredibly angry father who had stormed into my office, extremely upset with an interaction he had with his son's teacher. He was clenching and unclenching his fists, seething with anger. As I invited him to sit down, I took a few centering breaths. Turning my full attention and energy to him, I listened. Although I was aware of my shortness of breath and my rapid pulse, I calmed myself through *belly breathing*. I was conscious of not interrupting or judging him, instead giving him the time and space to express his feelings. I kept my body turned toward him, making eye contact and nodding when appropriate, and remained completely present as he spoke, not allowing my other tasks and duties to take away my attention. I treated him as if he was the most important person in the world. When he finished, I took a few mindful breaths. I shared with him that I understood his feelings, explaining that I, too, was a parent. Using different words, I shared with him what I had heard him express and asked him to clarify a few of his remarks. We came to a resolution that satisfied him, and I shook his hand as he left, thanking him for trusting us with educating his son.

Later that day, he came back by my office. This time, his demeanor was completely different. He thanked me for listening to his earlier "rant," and asked what kind of "magic" I had used on him. He admitted he came in extremely angry and left feeling he and his son both needed to apologize to the teacher. Although not every situation I handled as an educational leader worked out this smoothly, the "magic" the father referred to was *mindful listening*. Mindfulness is truly a gift you give to yourself and others.

This is the second book I have written about mindfulness. The first, *Cultivating Mindfulness in the Classroom* (2017), I wrote to offer educators tools to help themselves and their students. This book is written to serve as a mindfulness guide tailored specifically for educational leaders. Based on my over three decades as a mindfulness practitioner, over two decades as an educational leader, and five years as a mindfulness teacher and researcher, I have written this book to help leaders nurture themselves and others through the "magic" of mindful leadership.

Why Mindful Leadership

Educational leaders give so much of themselves in serving others. This includes nonstop problem solving, listening, leading, guiding, goal setting, and much more. Their leadership expertise and people skills are required when working with students, parents, staff members, other leaders, board members, and the public. Many leaders feel like hamsters endlessly running on a hamster wheel—exhausted and depleted. Many begin to feel like *human doings* rather than *human beings*.

Mindful leadership is a state of *being* rather than a state of *doing*. It occurs when we are fully present in conversations and listening to truly hear what another is saying, as opposed to planning our own response. It emphasizes compassion, both toward ourselves and others. It manifests itself as a state of equanimity, where there is a sense of mental calmness and evenness, even during difficult times. In a career as demanding and fast-paced as school leadership, leading mindfully helps leaders connect with themselves and others by slowing down enough to be present with *what is* both at school and home. This present-moment awareness helps leaders be open to the here and now, rather than regretting incidents in the past or having anxiety about future events.

The purpose of *Mindfulness First* is to provide you, as a school leader or district administrator, with a thorough guide for incorporating mindfulness and mindful leadership both personally and professionally. It provides an overview of mindfulness and mindful leadership, coupled with research-based strategies to help you develop mindfulness and strengthen your leadership. Let's get off the hamster wheel! To live and lead in a state of *being* rather than a state of *doing* is the essence of this book.

About This Book

Use *Mindfulness First* as a guide to developing and strengthening your mindfulness practice. While it may be tempting to jump from chapter to chapter based on your interest in a given topic, the practices I outline in this book build on one another, and I recommend moving through the chapters consecutively. Toward the end of each of this book's four chapters, you will find reflection questions. It is important to pause and consider your responses to these questions before progressing to the next chapter. These purposeful pauses offer you time to reflect on your understanding of the material presented. Take a moment to reread if necessary to deepen your understanding.

Chapter 1 provides an overview of the *what* and *why* of mindful leadership. Examine this chapter to develop an understanding of the meaning of mindfulness and mindful leadership, as well as the neuroscience that supports these concepts. The chapter describes attitudes that support mindful school leadership and further explains the benefits specific to the workplace.

From there, chapter 2 advises that leaders should *begin within* by first discovering mindfulness strategies they can practice on their own. This chapter details numerous practices you can develop personally, including mindful breathing, mindful meditation, and self-compassion. Through these practices, you will cultivate a sense of centeredness and peacefulness you can then extend to your leadership. This chapter includes fictional vignettes based on real-life examples to illustrate how you might use each technique during the school day or at home.

Once feeling centered and at peace, you, as a leader, can begin to *reach out* to others in mindfulness, which is the essence of chapter 3. Mindfulness is a powerful practice that can transform leadership. Mindful leaders reside in and exude calmness and presence in profound ways. This chapter details mindfulness tools specific to leading a community of educators, including mindful listening, mindful speaking, and ways to have difficult conversations mindfully. It again uses vignettes to illustrate how to use the mindfulness practices in your everyday life.

After learning about the various mindfulness practices you can implement to increase your personal mindfulness as well as reach out to others, you will likely be questioning how to put these strategies to use in real life. Chapter 4 provides a nine-week implementation plan you can use as a precise guide or a general recommendation. This chapter offers helpful reproducible tools, providing space for you to detail your personal commitments to mindfulness, as well as your reflections on each practice.

The book concludes with an appendix rife with recommended resources to help you continue to strengthen your mindfulness practice.

Time for Mindfulness

Leaders are often overwhelmed with responsibilities. As a leader, you feel the weight and stress of never-ending demands. You may often obsess over whether the many decisions you make each day are the right ones, serving both teacher and staff needs and, primarily, the needs and learning of students. With what feels like an unmanageable list of competing priorities, it's understandable to ask where you might find the time to learn about and practice mindfulness. And it's true—mindfulness does take practice, a consistent and daily dedication of giving time to yourself. Here's the reality: the more dedicated the practice, the better the results. At first, finding time to practice may seem like another task on your seemingly endless to-do list. With consistency, however, mindfulness can become as normal as brushing your teeth twice a day.

Some tips I have found for finding time for mindfulness include the following.

- Remember that mindfulness practice is something you do for yourself, rather than another chore to cross off your list (Kabat-Zinn, 1994). With a myriad benefits for both you and your leadership practice, it's easy to find time to do it because you *want* to find time.

- Practice mindful meditation before coffee! As I'm writing this, I've meditated for 444 consecutive days. The best way for me to make mindfulness a part of my everyday life is to connect it to another love of my life—coffee!

- Ask your administrative assistant to help you carve out precious mindfulness moments throughout your day. A school leader's time is rarely scripted, but you can let your assistant know that before meetings, you need five minutes to prepare. Use this time to breathe mindfully—try box breathing or belly breathing, which I describe later in this book. Also use this time to become keenly aware of your intentions for the meeting.

- Bookend your mindfulness. While the middle of the day might be full of interruptions, leaders are much more in control of the very beginning of the day and the time right before going to sleep. Use both "bookends" of your day to carve in mindfulness practices. Perhaps start your day with intention setting, which I describe later in this book. You may want to end your day with self-reflection and mindful meditation. You can accomplish each in five to fifteen minutes. The time you invest will pay off with dividends.

- Find a mindfulness buddy. A dear friend of mine, who is a school counselor, and I text each other every day with the number of minutes for our mindful meditation, as well as any other mindfulness practices we've implemented. This simple act reminds us both of practices we may have forgotten, as well as the importance of our consistent practice.

Although this book provides numerous formal mindfulness practices, it is important to note that you can integrate mindfulness informally into nearly everything you do. It is about bringing awareness to what you are doing with all your senses. It is possible to be mindful while showering, brushing your teeth, washing the dishes, and petting the dog. It is about being present in the moment in whatever you are doing. As John Kabat-Zinn (2005b), renowned teacher of mindfulness and founder of Mindfulness-Based Stress Reduction (MBSR) program, wrote in his poem "Tasting Mindfulness," it is about "being in your life *so completely*" (emphasis added).

You've been called to school leadership—and what an amazing calling! I've walked a mile in your shoes. I know how challenging our profession is. Trust me when I say practicing mindful leadership makes a deeper impact. By reading and implementing the mindfulness practices in this book, you will cultivate your ability to be more authentic, present, and compassionate toward yourself and those you serve.

CHAPTER 1

Understanding the *What* and *Why* of Mindful School Leadership

Mindfulness is the miracle by which we master and restore ourselves.

—Thich Nhat Hanh

School leadership is an incredibly difficult, complex, and demanding profession. Whether nurturing student needs, evaluating the effectiveness of educators, motivating stakeholders toward shared goals, or working with difficult parents, the demands are endless, and the hours are long. A study by the RAND Corporation revealed 85 percent of principals feel stress due to their job and 48 percent suffer from burnout. Twenty-eight percent have depressive symptoms (Steiner, Doan, Woo, Gittens, Lawrence, Berdie et al., 2022). Further, during the peak of the COVID-19 pandemic, only one-third of principals were satisfied with their role as leader of their school (National Association of Secondary School Principals, 2021). Granted, this situation was unique to a set of times and circumstances, but leaders still felt ill-equipped to do their jobs well or even adequately. The immense amount of stress and depressive symptoms of principals affects staff and students as well. It is difficult, if not impossible, to care for others if you do not first care for yourself. Each student and staff member deserves to have a well-balanced, peace-filled school leader.

It is understandably difficult to maintain a sense of peacefulness in the midst of the daily chaos of running a school, and few leaders receive training in self-care when studying to become a school leader. Wouldn't it be nice if you could make an inner shift that would improve your leadership capabilities while providing a sense of peacefulness and calmness? That is precisely where mindful school leadership comes in. This chapter first defines *mindfulness* and *mindful school leadership* before providing an overview of the history of mindfulness and its applications across several different fields of work. It describes the neuroscience of mindfulness, including how mindfulness practices interact with chemicals in the brain to create desirable outcomes. It then presents seven attitudes that support mindful school leadership, as well as the benefits of mindfulness in the workplace, to inspire and motivate you as you discover the mindfulness practices in the remainder of the book.

Mindfulness Defined

The term *mindfulness* means having present-moment awareness, being focused on both the task at hand and having an awareness of one's experience. Kabat-Zinn (1994) clarified that "mindfulness means paying attention in a particular way: on purpose, in the present moment, and nonjudgmentally" (p. 4).

In essence, mindfulness is about observing yourself without criticizing; it includes compassionate awareness toward yourself and others. Mindful individuals learn to treat disparaging thoughts with curiosity rather than dwell on stress. They begin to notice negative thoughts and let them go without giving in to negative thought patterns. When you are mindful:

> You are present for life and your experience just as it is . . . not as you hoped it would be, not as you expected it to be, not seeing more or less than what is here, not with judgments that can lead you to a conditioned reaction . . . but for exactly what is here, as it unfolds, meeting each moment with equanimity. (Marturano, 2014, p. 8)

In a school environment, a mindful state of being allows leaders to truly listen to understand, accept the current reality, and thoughtfully respond to what is. When chaos arrives in your school, as it inevitably will, mindful leadership takes you away from automatic reactions and into responsiveness. It allows you to slow down and zoom out to view challenges from a broader perspective, staying open to possibilities.

It is important to dispel a few myths about mindfulness.

- Mindfulness is different from meditation, the latter of which *supports* mindfulness. *Meditation* is sustained awareness of an object, such as the breath—an intentional practice that enhances and supports mindfulness. *Mindfulness* includes but is not limited to meditation (Iberlin, 2017). Rather, it is inclusive of many activities and strategies.

- Mindfulness is not inherently a religious activity (Iberlin, 2017). Religious people and atheists alike can practice it effectively.

- Mindfulness is not time consuming (Iberlin, 2017). It does, however, require patience and dedication. Over time, mindfulness improves overall well-being by reducing stress, rumination, and anxiety. Mindfulness helps you be present in the here and now, which can lead to increased enjoyment of life's pleasures and greater acceptance of life's difficulties.

- Mindfulness is not expensive. In fact, you can implement mindfulness practices anytime, anywhere, at no cost. Many of the mindfulness apps referenced in the appendix are free (Iberlin, 2017)!

- Mindfulness is not a substitute for medical treatment. Individuals should consult a medical professional for ongoing negative feelings, including major depression, unresolved trauma, and suicidal ideation.

- Mindfulness is not a silver bullet or cure-all response to stress. Rather, it is a tool that helps people see the world with greater clarity, allowing them to change what needs to change.

- Mindfulness does not numb the mind or give people a *Pollyanna attitude* (a positivity bias). Rather, mindfulness serves as an aid in helping you accept reality as opposed to being swept up by too much positivity *or* negativity.

- Mindfulness is not another chore to cross off a to-do list. It is something people do for themselves, with benefits for both themselves and others (Kabat-Zinn, 1994).

With the rising popularity of mindfulness, it is important to understand these misconceptions. Although mindfulness may not be a fit for everyone, I encourage you to give mindfulness a dedicated try. Mindfulness practices have the ability to bring you more peace, compassion, and joy, improving your overall well-being. Remember, during your practice, mindfulness is not a destination; it is a journey. This practice has the potential to enhance both your personal life and your life as a school leader. This is the intersection between mindfulness and leadership, known as *mindful leadership.*

Mindful leadership is defined as "a leadership practice focused on cultivating very high levels of self-awareness, wisdom, and self-mastery, allowing a leader to bring his or her best self to all aspects of leadership and daily life, and to inspire greatness in others" (Tenney, 2022). It includes being responsive rather than reactive, listening with presence, and regulating your emotions. Some may consider mindful leadership another task that takes too much time; however, the time and effort reap numerous rewards. The time you invest in the practice of mindful leadership leaves you better able to navigate the barrage of demands and deepen the connections in the myriad relationships of a school leader.

A mindful school leader shows up with more presence and openness. Imagine a new teacher, Martha, meeting you for the first time. As a mindful school leader, you make sure Martha becomes the most important person *in that moment*, no matter what other tasks are pressing. You give her the gift of your time by being fully present, as opposed to checking your smartphone or silently planning the next tasks to cross off your to-do list. With eye contact, engaged posture, and authentic interest, you ask questions to get to know Martha both personally and professionally. You share the school's vision and explain how she fits into that vision. Martha leaves feeling valued and connected. You feel present, unrushed, peaceful, and connected to a valuable member of the school team.

A mindful school leader conducts staff meetings with presence and open-mindedness. Instead of coming in with all the answers and an agenda to sell, a mindful school leader values each person's insight and input. A mindful school leader asks questions and listens with curiosity and openness. This style of leadership allows all stakeholders to feel valued and part of the team contributing to students' learning and overall well-being.

Although most school-related mindfulness research has been conducted to show the beneficial effects of mindfulness for students, research also supports mindfulness for school leaders and teachers. A study of thirteen school administrators, who had participated in a mindfulness professional development program, revealed improved leadership skills, including strengthened relationships and increased self-reflection. Participants also enhanced their ability to recognize and regulate their own emotions (Mahfouz, 2018). Similarly, mindfulness training has been shown to improve teaching by helping teachers self-regulate their emotions and manage stress. In a study of 113 public school teachers, participants found mindfulness training beneficial.

The participants reported improved attention, deeper self-compassion, and lower levels of stress (Roeser, Schonert-Reichl, Jha, Cullen, Wallace, Wilensky et al., 2013). Although further research is needed, mindfulness is showing it has a role in both teaching and school leadership.

History and Applications of Mindfulness

Mindfulness, which is gaining popularity in schools and for leadership, has a noteworthy history. It is important to understand that mindfulness is international. It derived from monks, meditation teachers, practitioners, doctors, and many others. This book discusses a secular and scientific approach to mindfulness; however, the term is rooted in both Hindu and Buddhist practices (Iberlin, 2017).

The concept of mindfulness is old. The concept of mindfulness can be traced back to the Pali word *sati*, which refers to the state of being aware and alert (Wilson, 2014). Mindfulness has been practiced for over 2,500 years and began to take root in America in the early 1900s. Its popularity increased in the 1960s, when numerous Buddhists from Thailand and Vietnam moved to the United States. America's first Buddhist temple was established in 1965 in Washington, DC, bringing about a greater acceptance of Buddhist practices (Wilson, 2014). Then, in 1979, Jack Kornfield, Sharon Salzberg, and Joseph Goldstein founded the Insight Meditation Center. After practicing Buddhism in South Asia, they wanted to bring mindfulness practices to the West. They downplayed chanting, cosmology, and ceremony, turning their focus instead to mindfulness and meditation (Wilson, 2014). Perhaps the most influential figure for introducing mindfulness to the mainstream culture is Kabat-Zinn (2013), who developed and taught the MBSR program. He founded the MBSR Clinic in 1979, introducing mindfulness as a way to reduce stress and quiet the mind (Kabat-Zinn, 2005a).

The benefits of mindfulness are becoming evident in many different mainstream fields and companies. Prominent businesses and well-known individuals have implemented mindfulness practices to boost both productivity and mental health. Google, for example, has provided mindfulness training to its employees since 2007 (Tan, 2012). Chade-Meng Tan, a Google employee, leads the teaching of mindfulness to staff. Although Google offers dozens of mindfulness courses, the most popular course is called Search Inside Yourself. Based on the core areas of engaging in attention training, learning self-knowledge and self-mastery, and creating useful mental habits, the seven-week course garners rave reviews from participants, who reported being calmer, more patient, and better able to deal with stress and grief (Tan, 2012). The company's Search Inside Yourself training is still offered, and a new program called gPause evolved from it and serves as an avenue for peer-led weekly and biweekly meetings to offer colleagues support in mindfulness practices (Gensler, 2021).

Another well-known company to offer mindfulness training is Aetna, an American-managed healthcare company. In 2010, Aetna launched two mindfulness programs, Mindfulness at Work and Viniyoga Stress Reduction, to help reduce employees' stress. Participants showed improvements in their stress levels and heart rate measurements. Aetna liked the outcomes of the programs so much that it began offering them to customers (Goguen-Hughes, 2011). General Mills, Intel, Target, and Green Mountain Roasters also offer mindfulness programs for their employees (Schaufenbuel, 2015). These businesses attest that mindfulness has improved people's listening skills, stress levels, focus, and overall well-being.

Sports are yet another area to benefit from leadership including mindfulness programs. Several NFL teams have adopted mindfulness programs, including the Seattle Seahawks, Indianapolis Colts, San Francisco 49ers, and Atlanta Falcons (Neporent, 2014). When Pete Carroll, the head coach of the Seahawks, began coaching the team, his goal was to improve the team's psychological readiness. He relied on Michael Gervais, the team's sports psychologist, to teach the players to meditate for just a few minutes each day. As they became more proficient in mindfulness, the players meditated for longer periods of time. Mindfulness helped players better manage their thoughts (Neporent, 2014). These benefits were also apparent with other teams, many of whom adopted similar practices. Dan Quinn, the former head coach of the Falcons, stated:

> Some people might think using meditation and having a mental performance side might soften you up, but it's just the opposite. It allows you to experience yourself the way you'd like to be. We think of ourselves as a tough-ass, hard-nosed team. But when we have a chance to apply some of this mental training, it helps with football, but it also helps off the field quite a bit too. (as cited in Mays, 2017)

Mindfulness is highly relevant to the military as well. Mindfulness provides soldiers with tools to help them feel less stressed and more positive about life, whether in training, active duty, or the post-deployment transition back to home life. A 2011 study of 160 United States Marines showed mindfulness training better prepares soldiers for high-stress combat situations, as well as improving cognition and resilience (Stanley, Schaldach, Kiyonaga, & Jha, 2011). Soldiers learned about focused attention, breath awareness, and physical awareness of the body. Following the training, participants were exposed to stimuli, including the sights, sounds, and smells they would experience in deployment. Participants showed a quicker recovery in their breathing and heart rate when compared to a control group that did not receive the mindfulness training. The mindful marines also had a better quality of sleep without nightmares (Stanley et al., 2011). The U.S. Army is also benefiting from mindfulness training. Major General Walter E. Piatt led army soldiers stationed in Hawaii to start implementing mindfulness practices to improve their shooting skills. Specifically, mindfulness helped the soldiers know when to pull the trigger during chaotic times to protect civilians from harm (Richtel, 2019). Mindfulness training has also proven to be helpful for military veterans who served in Afghanistan and Iraq. Using a breathing-based mindfulness technique, veteran participants showed a reduction in post-traumatic stress disorder (PTSD), respiration rates, and anxiety, while the control group did not (Seppälä, Nitschke, Tudorascu, Hayes, Goldstein, Nguyen et al., 2014).

The widespread adaptation of mindfulness is likely due to the impact mindfulness practices have on the way people feel and think. I will discuss the *neuroscience of mindfulness*—its biological impact on the brain—in the following section.

Neuroscience of Mindfulness

The benefits of mindfulness practice link to the neuroplasticity of the human brain. *Neuroplasticity* is when the brain adapts and reorganizes neural pathways from new experiences (Puderbaugh & Emmady, 2022). Through neuroplasticity, you can rewire and change your brain (Puderbaugh & Emmady, 2022). When an experience repeats, neurons wire together, creating a quicker and easier response. Put another way:

> A good metaphor for neurons wiring together is a sled sliding down a snowy hill. During the initial ride down the hill, a sled might travel at an average speed; but, if the sled follows the same path on the second run, it will travel faster because the snow has been compressed. (Iberlin, 2017, p. 10)

Over time, practicing mindfulness positively changes the brain's pathways related to reducing stress, managing attention, regulating emotions, and improving mood.

In conjunction with knowledge of how neurons behave, mindfulness practices can literally change the ways people think and feel. Health and wellness expert Maggie Seaver (2020) states:

> We have more control over our thoughts and behaviors than we think. While the brain does adapt on its own, we know there are ways to take matters into our own hands: to awaken, strengthen, create, and even rewire certain neural pathways intentionally in order to boost brain function and overall health.

Mindfulness and mindful meditation impact the way human bodies and brains respond to events. Life events release hormones and neurotransmitters that act as chemical messengers across the body and brain (Sousa, 2011). Several studies reveal that mindful meditation specifically increases the following three *feel-good* neurotransmitters.

- **Endorphins:** Mindful meditation releases endorphins as well as increases feel-good chemicals, including serotonin, dopamine, and melatonin. One study showed *endorphins*, a type of neurotransmitter responsible for creating a sense of happiness, were more elevated in highly trained meditators than in a group of elite runners following a session of meditation and running, respectively (Curtin, 2014). Therefore, people can also attain the state of bliss runners often describe as a *runner's high* through meditation.

- **Gamma-aminobutyric acid (GABA):** *GABA* is known for creating a sense of calmness, and not having enough of this chemical can result in anxiety, racing thoughts, and sleeplessness (Guglietti, Daskalakis, Radhu, Fitzgerald, & Ritvo, 2013). A study by the Boston University School of Medicine found a 27 percent increase in GABA levels after sixty minutes of mindful meditation (as cited in Guglietti et al., 2013).

- **Serotonin:** This neurotransmitter induces calmness and regulates mood, and has also been found to increase after meditation. Long-term meditators are shown to have high levels of serotonin (Newberg & Iverson, 2003).

The release of neurotransmitters and the brain's neuroplasticity allow mindfulness practitioners to experience both short- and long-term effects.

The list of neurological changes that occur through mindful meditation doesn't stop with neurotransmitters. A meta-analysis of neuroimaging of three hundred brains revealed the following eight regions of the brain changed through meditation (Fox, Nijeboer, Dixon, Floman, Ellamil, Rumak et al., 2014).

1. *Corpus callosum*, an area that communicates between the brain's hemispheres

2. *Superior longitudinal fasciculus*, also an area that communicates between the brain's hemispheres

3. *Mid-cingulate cortex*, an area connected with self-regulation and attention

4. *Anterior cingulate cortex*, an area also associated with self-control and attention

5. *Hippocampus*, an area involved forming memories and emotional responses

6. *Insular cortex*, an area involved in tactile information such as body awareness and pain

7. *Sensory cortices*, areas that also involve tactile information

8. *Rostrolateral prefrontal cortex*, an area linked with *meta-awareness* (thinking about the thinking process) and introspection

Although the meta-analysis revealed some differences between the varied studies, there was consistency in the changes in the brain. These include changes in brain density, thickness of brain tissue, the number of neurons and fibers, and changes in both the cortical surface area and white-matter fiber density (Fox et al., 2014). Simply put, mindful meditation can literally change your brain for the better. All you need is little time and space to develop this practice. With consistent practice, your brain can literally rewire itself.

A 2011 study by Harvard affiliates at the Massachusetts General Hospital also revealed structural changes in the density of *gray matter* in the brain, which is the part of the brain that influences stress, mood, and attention (Hölzel, Carmody, Vangel, Congleton, Yerramsetti, Gard et al., 2011). Researchers studied participants' brains before and after undergoing the eight-week MBSR program, which Kabat-Zinn (2003) developed in 1979. They found increased gray matter in the *hippocampus*, which relates to emotional regulation and corresponding decrease in gray matter in the *amygdala*, a structure in the brain related to stress, anxiety, and the fight-or-flight response. The researchers concluded that through mindfulness practice, you can reduce stress not by eliminating it but by changing out-of-proportion reactions to stress (Hölzel et al., 2011).

Research on mindfulness, although still in its infancy, reveals promising results for those who practice mindfulness and mindful meditation. Consistent mindfulness practice yields better results, but even small periods of daily practice can alter your brain (Keng, Smoski, & Robins, 2011). This means that through mindfulness practices including mindful meditation, you, as a school leader, will be in better control of your emotions, especially during highly stressful situations. You will also be more vigilant of the impact you have on other people through your words and actions.

Attitudes to Support Mindful School Leadership

The following fictional scenario paints one picture of a mindful school leader's attitudes and behaviors that you can develop over time.

A mindful school leader, Maya, begins her day with a mindful meditation in which she anchors herself by focusing on her in- and out-breaths. As concerns for the upcoming school day and grocery and to-do lists enter her awareness, Maya notices them and lets them go. Before exiting her car to enter the school, she sets an intention for the day: *to be truly present with students, staff, and parents.* To prepare for any difficult meetings, Maya takes time to center herself with a few cleansing breaths.

Maya intentionally sends feelings of compassion from her heart to those she is serving through her leadership. As she enters meetings, she brings both a sense of confidence and openness to what may arise. She resides in the sweet spot of trusting in her own talents and expertise as well as those of others. Before making impactful decisions, Maya takes time to listen and learn.

She knows human beings all make mistakes. Consequently, Maya shows grace toward others and herself. She also knows effective changes take time. Relationships truly matter to Maya; she treats each person she interacts with as if they are the most important person in her world. Instead of mindlessly attacking her to-do list, this mindful leader is open to varied possibilities for her day. Instead of being reactive, she is thoughtful and attentive.

Being a mindful school leader is not an easy feat. However, certain qualities go hand in hand with mindfulness and mindful leadership. Kabat-Zinn (2013) describes seven qualities that support mindfulness: (1) non-judging, (2) patience, (3) beginner's mind, (4) trust in oneself, (5) non-striving, (6) acceptance, and (7) letting go. Kabat-Zinn (2013) refers to these qualities as the *attitudinal foundations of mindfulness*, attitudes you can cultivate and strengthen throughout your workday and in your home. Because they are all interconnected, when you strengthen one, you also strengthen the others. Thus, cultivating these attitudes of the mind deepens your practice of mindful school leadership.

The following sections describe each of these seven attitudes in relation to mindfulness and mindful leadership. Through cultivating these attitudes of mindfulness in your heart and mind, a shift gradually occurs, moving you toward a more spacious, virtuous way of being. You may consider focusing first on the attitudes that most need your attention. Developing one or more of them naturally connects with the others and improves your overall mindfulness.

Non-Judging

Non-judging is developing an awareness of how judgmental you are. People often jump to liking or disliking this opinion or that idea without noticing how quickly they jumped to judgment. Non-judging means developing an awareness of your judgmental nature and not judging yourself for judging. Non-judging allows you to see yourself clearly through what you immediately choose to like or dislike.

As a leader, you may think non-judging seems virtually impossible. No matter what happens in your school, you are likely to notice when you have formed an opinion about events and experiences. For example, when interviewing a potential teacher, you may not even be aware of your biases based on your own past and history. This could allow you to forgo an amazing and talented educator because of your instant prejudgment. As you begin to notice your thoughts and emotions through your mindfulness practice, you may become aware that you are judging *everything*—constantly!

Such constant judgment—of experiences, events, other people, or even the objective information surrounding you—can lock you into habitual patterns of thinking and automatic responses. Mindful leadership allows you to consciously make decisions based on thoughtful reflection and input, whereas an automatic response relies on knee-jerk reactions and habits. Through mindfulness, you can live in a state of being alert and attentive to the people and events each day brings. A habitual reaction could be a closed response to your superintendent's feedback of your performance. "That jerk just criticized me. How can he not see my greatness?" is an example of the defenses people provide automatically. Mindfulness practice, on the other hand, can help you become aware you are judging. Kabat-Zinn (2013) encourages you not to judge your judging—you don't have to try to stop it, just notice it. As you learn to step back from habitual judging, you can then see things more clearly, allowing for more creative thinking and thoughtful responses.

Examples of Judging Versus Non-Judging Attitudes

Judging attitude: Andrew instinctually judges a student based on her older sibling's behaviors. No matter what the student has to say herself, Andrew assumes she is guilty as charged.

Non-judging attitude: First, Andrew develops an awareness of his tendency to jump to judgment. Once he notices his judgment, he breathes in deeply and lets the breath go, remembering not to judge himself for his feelings. Next, Andrew aims for open communication. He asks open-ended questions and truly listens. Instead of imposing a "good" or "right" response to the student's thoughts, he asks her what she thinks of her reactions or responses to the situation at hand. He tries to see the situation from the student's perspective instead of jumping in with his own point of view.

Judging attitude: A principal, Madeleine, quickly judges a teacher who claims his students will never meet the school's reading goals based on their previous year's placement in his classroom. Immediately, Madeleine sees this teacher as a failure for prejudging his students so quickly. She feels immediate hostility toward him and makes plans to visit his classroom often to confirm her belief that he lacks the can-do attitude.

Non-judging attitude: Madeleine gives herself some time to breathe. When she's in a calmer state of mind, she schedules a meeting with the teacher. During the meeting, she gives him time to share his specific concerns. Then, she tries to put herself in his shoes. How must it feel if his students do not make their annual reading goals? Once the teacher has his say, together the principal and teacher make a plan to help his students meet success. At the end of the meeting, Madeleine takes some time to reflect on the conversation. What went well? What needs readdressing at a later time?

Patience

Patience is an understanding that you simply cannot hurry certain things. It involves allowing things to unfold at their own pace. Instead of always hurrying to get to the next thing, you are open and present with where you are.

School leaders need immense patience. You cannot earn trust and respect from staff, students, parents, and colleagues overnight. Once you have earned trust and respect, you need patience to continue to nurture that trust and respect. Further, you need patience to not push teachers or students beyond their abilities. You achieve great and lasting results step by step.

Due to the nature of the demands on a school leader, you may often feel impatient. For example, before completing one meeting with a disgruntled parent, your mind may focus on the two students who got into a major fight during lunch. But when your attention is focused on a future task, you are not truly present for the task requiring your attention *now*.

By rushing from one task to the next, you can miss the heart of each moment. Practicing patience allows you to see that things unfold in their own time. Mindfulness practice can help you develop patience by allowing you to be present with each moment as it unfolds.

Examples of Impatient Versus Patient Attitudes

Impatient attitude: A sixth-grade teacher, Cami, exhibits all the qualities of great leadership but is unsure of her abilities. Her impatient leader strongly wants her to serve as the team leader for the sixth-grade pod regardless of her insecurities, as the only thing holding her back is her lack of belief in herself. Cami's leader increasingly reminds Cami of her responsibility to serve others and asks her not to be selfish.

Patient attitude: With the attitude of patience, a mindful school leader realizes Cami needs time to accept her gifts as a leader. The patient leader invites Cami to a one-to-one meeting to discuss her feelings. Rather than bringing a fixed agenda, the mindful leader listens with an open heart, asking guiding questions and making connections. Knowing it's not wise to push people beyond their capabilities, the patient leader plants seeds of confidence and belief in Cami.

Impatient attitude: A particularly disgruntled parent shows up often at the office and demands the principal's time. The impatient principal, David, accepts the parent into the office with an audible sigh. While glancing repeatedly at his cell phone, David looks occasionally at the parent. Shortly into the conversation, and right on cue, the administrative assistant buzzes in, alerting David about another (make-believe) meeting. The parent leaves, slamming the door behind him.

Patient attitude: David invites the disgruntled parent into the office and suppresses a sigh. Knowing this parent cares about his child, David puts his cell phone in a drawer and turns all of his attention to the parent. Bringing his attention to his breath, David settles in to listen. Making eye contact and giving truly thoughtful responses, he thanks the parent for expressing his concerns. Knowing he has another commitment soon, David offers the parent a time slot open the next day. Since the disgruntled parent feels heard and not rushed, he leaves with a thank-you and agrees to set another meeting time.

Beginner's Mind

Having a *beginner's mind* is seeing things as if for the first time. Many times, people restrict themselves by applying knowledge of past events or experiences and assuming it must apply in a new situation. For example, you might enter into a situation between a student and a teacher thinking you know all the answers already. Betsy, the ninth-grade algebra teacher, does not care for her student Rachel's attitude. Rachel sits in the back of Betsy's class refusing to take notes or answer any questions directed at her.

As an expert practitioner, you might label Rachel as defiant and uncooperative. However, these labels are truly unfair. You don't know Rachel's point of view or situation until you listen with openness. A beginner's mind asks you to look at the situation with fresh eyes. In reality, you have never been in this exact place before. The mindful leader brings openness to both the teacher and student, making sure they both feel seen and heard. As layers get peeled back through one-to-one meetings, it is revealed that two girls in her class are bullying Rachel. Rachel accuses the teacher of allowing this to go on. Rachel does not, however, want her teacher to overtly confront the girls about their behavior. Betsy, although feeling a bit defensive, listens carefully to the accusation. At the end of their meeting, Betsy agrees to be more vigilant to the happenings in the classroom. Rachel agrees to be more cooperative if the bullying stops. As this situation illustrates, a beginner's mind allows you to view a situation from a fresh perspective. While still taking into account past incidents, you are able to see new information more clearly.

As the famous quote by Zen master Shunryu Suzuki (2020) states, "In the beginner's mind, there are many possibilities, but in the expert's there are few" (p. 148). Each situation is unique. A beginner's mind allows you to be open to possibilities and viewpoints. This openness can lead school leaders to more creative and, often, more helpful solutions.

Examples of Expert Versus Beginner's Mind Attitudes

Expert attitude: It is time for the summative evaluation of Carl's employees. As the expert, Carl already knows and pinpoints the exact skills each employee needs to improve before meeting with each of them. In fact, his summative evaluations are already written. All the employees need to do is listen and then sign.

Beginner's mind attitude: Carl brings a beginner's mind to each interaction with others, even for evaluations. Instead of having all the answers at hand, he is curious about each employee's self-evaluation. What are the employee's ideas for improvement? What are the employee's solutions to any perceived obstacles? This openness to others' ideas and opinions allows Carl to see varied possibilities he may not have considered.

Expert attitude: As a veteran leader, Tania independently designs the opening staff meeting for the upcoming school year. After all, she has done this twenty times in her tenure. She expects last year's slide presentation will probably work just fine this year if she adds in a few new slides.

Beginner's mind attitude: Tania meets with her teacher leaders and other teachers and staff members available over the summer. She asks for the input of others and shows her vulnerability. Tania

▶

admits she doesn't have all the answers and needs and values their input. During the various meetings, Tania intentionally sets aside her notions and truly listens. She is looking for possibilities she has not yet considered. This level of vulnerability allows Tania to have more authentic connections with her staff.

Trust in Oneself

Learning to *trust in oneself* is an integral part of mindful leadership and a powerful attitude to cultivate. Trust in yourself means trusting your inner voice and intuition. This includes believing in your ability to meet any challenges that arise.

People reside in the belief they can meet challenges. There is a distinct difference between trusting in yourself and having an expert attitude. Trusting in yourself does not mean you have all the answers. Your trust is believing you can and will find the answers in your experiences and openness to others' ideas and opinions.

Too often people believe knowledge is "out there," overlooking the powerful resource of their own being. If you lack self-trust, you may tend to forgo your decisions if there is any resistance or pushback. For example, Gerry, a high school principal, has made the decision to begin school an hour later to allow high school students adequate time for sleep. He made this decision with a team of educators and parents who researched teenagers' need for sleep. However, numerous staff members expressed resistance to this decision. Lacking self-trust, Gerry abandoned the decision against his better judgment, stating he and the team would look into it again the next school year. Because he was plagued with self-doubt, Gerry was unable to stand behind the team's decision. As a school leader, you have a wealth of knowledge and tremendous resources within you. If something doesn't seem right to you, trust your inner guidance. At times you may make mistakes, but by trusting your inner guidance, you will generally make the right decisions.

To be an impactful leader, trust in oneself is necessary. Through learning to trust yourself, you become more fully yourself. Mindfulness practice can help you develop self-trust. By sitting with yourself and noticing your thoughts and emotions, you deepen your understanding of yourself.

Examples of Lacking Self-Trust Versus Trust in Oneself Attitudes

Lacking self-trust attitude: As a school leader, Rebecca has misinterpreted students' test results while making a presentation to educators. Lacking self-trust, Rebecca severely criticizes herself and labels herself incompetent and unintelligent.

Trust in oneself attitude: Trusting in herself, Rebecca acknowledges her error and apologizes for the mistake. She makes a plan to go over data more carefully in the future. She realizes mistakes happen, and she lets it go and moves on.

Lacking self-trust attitude: Jerome has a tough conversation ahead of him to non-renew an educator. The educator has been extremely aggressive toward students in both actions and words and has not improved after several warnings. Throughout the conversation with the teacher, Jerome is filled with self-doubt. He continually wonders if he's doing the right thing in regard to the teacher's non-renewal.

Trust in oneself attitude: Jerome centers himself with a few deep breaths. He then brings to mind the most important principles of educating students. As he has the difficult conversation with the teacher, Jerome knows he has the strength to stand up for students by not allowing this teacher to continue to serve as an educator.

Non-Striving

At the core of mindfulness is the idea of *non-striving*. It simply means *being with what is* as opposed to *constantly doing*. For example, Juan, a high school principal, keeps a long to-do list on his smartphone. Knowing much of his focus is on *doing*, he incorporates time outside work and during his workday to simply *be*. This includes starting his day with meditation and including mindful breathing throughout his day. Juan takes purposeful pauses to just engage with others, not looking for what is "right" or "wrong," but simply being with them.

When you are constantly striving, you have difficulty being at ease. As you develop your mindfulness practice, you may find yourself striving for peace. This striving undermines the essence of mindfulness, which is paying attention to the here and now, just as it is. An attitude of non-striving can serve a school administrator well. It allows you to step out of the *doing* mode and ease into the *being* mode. As a result, you will be more present and self-aware in both your home and work lives.

Examples of Striving Versus Non-Striving Attitudes

Striving attitude: As Carolina begins her mindfulness practices, she finds herself literally striving for peace. She becomes attached to the outcome of feeling centered and peaceful. She judges herself and her mindfulness practice if she isn't able to access these feelings in every session.

Non-striving attitude: During her mindfulness practice, Carolina notices that she is striving. She does not judge herself for striving. She notices it, and then she practices letting the striving go.

Acceptance

Acceptance is the realization that a situation is what it is—at least for the moment. It doesn't mean you don't try to improve the situation or make things better in the school setting; rather, it is about seeing things in the moment as they actually are. It does not mean resignation; rather, when you have a clear picture of the current moment, you are more likely to know how to make improvements going forward instead of operating from a place of fear or clouded vision.

For example, imagine a situation of school bullying. Preventing school bullying has been one of your school's priorities for several years, and your leadership team has implemented several interventions. However, an honest look at the data might indicate that several interventions have failed to make an impact on bullying in the school. It takes courage to accept these data—indeed, it would be wonderful to be able to say the opposite, that the interventions are working exactly as planned! However, that rosy attitude will do little to help the students involved as both bullies and those being bullied. Only by clearly seeing and accepting the reality of the current situation can you and your staff begin to make the needed improvements.

Mindfulness practice helps you strengthen your acceptance of the way things are. Through mindfulness, you are open to your thoughts, feelings, and emotions just as they are in the moment. You do not judge them, but instead, witness them. If you can clearly see what is in front of you, you can make the needed changes. Developing your levels of acceptance will clearly help you become a more mindful school leader.

Examples of Non-Accepting Versus Accepting Attitudes

Non-accepting attitude: Several teachers have come forward to express their concerns about staff negativity. Feeling defensive and responsible for their concerns, their principal, Kenji, states he has not witnessed negativity in staff members. He simply denies the teachers' claims.

Accepting attitude: As a mindful school leader, Kenji acknowledges the teachers' concerns about the negative tone in staff members. By accepting that negativity is happening in the school, Kenji and the team of educators can then take actions to make changes.

Letting Go

Kabat-Zinn (2013) defines *letting go* as "a way of letting things be, of accepting things as they are" (p. 30). It is not clinging to feelings you'd like to keep and pushing away strong and painful emotions. Although it's natural to want to hold on to positive emotions and good feelings, if you try to push away the feelings that hurt you, you find yourself in conflict with what is actually hurting you. Both clinging to false positive feelings and pushing away negative feelings can ultimately cause you more suffering than good.

For example, people all appreciate the feeling of being liked. However, as a school administrator, you also know not everyone will like you. Although it is human nature to cling to the idea of wanting to be liked by everyone and fixating on those who don't like you, this actually causes suffering. When you understand that clinging to such desires is painful, you can let these desires go. Letting go is an opening to experiencing freedom from desires and clinging.

Examples of Clinging Versus Letting Go Attitudes

Clinging attitude: As a school leader, Evelyn has a tendency toward perfectionism. Her high standards are part of what allows her to achieve at high levels. Evelyn displays a clinging attitude, showing self-loathing for not being perfect or for making mistakes.

Letting go attitude: Evelyn is aware of her tendency to value perfection in all she does. Whenever such feelings arise, she repeats a mantra she has written on a sticky note and placed next to her computer: "*Done* is better than *perfect.*" With practice, Evelyn has learned to accept that mistakes will come and that she needs to let go of the desire to be perfect all the time.

Benefits of Workplace Mindfulness

Grounded in the roots of mindfulness, mindful leadership provides many benefits for you as a leader and for those you lead. Based on their extensive work with educational leaders, coauthors Valerie Brown and Kristin Olsen (2015) cite the following benefits of mindfulness for leaders:

- Improved ability to notice and slow down, or stop, automatic reactions (p. 10)
- Increased capacity to respond to complex and difficult situations (p. 11)
- Ability to see situations more clearly, or many dimensions of a situation (p. 11)
- Becoming more creative at designing complex dilemmas (p. 11)
- Ability to achieve balance and greater resilience at work and at home (p. 12)

Leaders who are mindful are less reactive (Goldin & Gross, 2010), and have improved emotional intelligence (Charoensukmongkol, 2014) and increased compassion (Shapiro, Brown, & Biegel, 2007). Mindfulness helps leaders be more intentional and have greater focus on the task at hand. It helps them thrive in the workplace in spite of the conflicts and stresses of day-to-day life. Table 1.1 highlights these numerous benefits of mindfulness (selected because of their relevancy to the workplace) and the supporting research.

TABLE 1.1: Benefits of Mindfulness Practices Relevant to the Workplace and the Supporting Research

Benefits of Mindfulness Practices Relevant to the Workplace	Supporting Research
Decreased anxiety	Biegel, Brown, Shapiro, & Schubert, 2009; Tacón, McComb, Caldera, & Randolph, 2003
Reduced conflict	University of British Columbia, 2018
Reduced emotional exhaustion	Hülsheger, Alberts, Feinholdt, & Lang, 2013
Improved stress management	Branstrom, Kvillemo, Brandberg, & Moskowitz, 2010; Chiesa & Serretti, 2009; Hyland, Lee, & Mills, 2015; Shapiro, Astin, Bishop, & Cordova, 2005
Improved empathy	Block-Lerner, Adair, Plumb, Rhatigan, & Orsillo, 2007; Siegel, 2010; Winning & Boag, 2015
Increased emotional regulation	Guendelman, Medeiros, & Rampes, 2017; Siegel, 2007
Improved cognitive focus	Chambers, Gullone, & Allen, 2009; Whitfield et al., 2022
Increased working memory	Chambers, Lo, & Allen, 2008; Jha, Stanley, Kiyonaga, Wong, & Gelfand, 2010
Improved emotional intelligence	Charoensukmongkol, 2014
Improved social relationships	Cohen & Miller, 2009; Giluk, 2010; Glomb, Duffy, Bono, & Yang, 2012; Hülsheger et al., 2013
Increased focus	Panskepp & Biven, 2012; Schonert-Reichl & Lawlor, 2010
Increased optimism	Schonert-Reichl & Lawlor, 2010
Increased willingness to help others	Hafenbrack et al., 2020
Increased self-determination and persistence	Glomb et al., 2012
Greater enjoyment in work	Hyland et al., 2015

Although the benefits of mindfulness practices in the workplace are many, school leaders face specific challenges relating to their work, and mindfulness practices can benefit school leaders in unique ways. In the following sections, I provide more detail regarding how mindfulness can particularly benefit school leaders in the areas of (1) decreased stress, (2) improved emotional intelligence, and (3) improved social relationships.

Decreased Stress

Stress is a "physical, mental and emotional response to a challenging event. . . . The stress response occurs automatically when you feel threatened" (Mayo Clinic Staff, 2022b). Stress is a normal part of the life of an administrator, but over time, chronic stress can lead to harmful physical responses, such as depression and risk of heart disease. Left unaided, chronic stress can also lead to higher blood pressure, increased cortisol levels, and increased heart rate (Mayo Clinic Staff, 2022b). Mindfulness lowers stress by helping you stay in the present moment, consequently controlling racing thoughts that can increase stress. Further, mindfulness practices help you be with what is before you. Instead of identifying with your negative thoughts and emotions, through mindfulness you learn to *witness* them. You can realize they are just passing thoughts, feelings, or emotions. The act of witnessing protects you from outside stressors.

Although many occupations are stressful, including many roles in education, educational leadership is a uniquely high-stress position. The decisions leaders make can result in staff turnover or educator burnout that then affects all other individuals in the building—students in particular. A well-intentioned but misguided leadership decision can negatively impact learning in any number of ways. In a study at The Pennsylvania State University, researchers found the role of principal is becoming increasingly stressful: "Reflecting the high stress and low support associated with the position, principals in urban schools remain in their positions for just three to four years, which is often not long enough to impact their school's success" (Mahfouz, Greenberg, & Rodriguez, 2019). Further, coauthors Angus S. Mungal and Richard Sorenson (2021) found the common sources of stressors for principals include:

- Excessive demands and responsibilities
- Absence of supervisory support and/or fellow principal networking
- Lack of control over campus-related decisions
- Constant problem-solving dilemmas
- Conflicting or unclear performance expectations

Mungal and Sorenson (2021) emphasized implementing relaxation techniques, and Mahfouz and colleagues (2019) emphasized the urgent need for principals to prioritize their own social and emotional well-being, including through mindfulness interventions and emotional intelligence training.

A further source of stress was the COVID-19 pandemic and subsequent need to move education to remote classes, often with little notice. In a study of over one thousand school leaders in New York City, researchers found school leaders were feeling a great deal of stress:

Leaders were asked to share the three emotions they had experienced the most during the prior two weeks. An overwhelming 95 percent of the feelings they named could be classified as "negative." The most commonly mentioned emotion was anxiety, which stood out glaringly above all others—overwhelmed, sad, stressed, frustrated, uncertain, and worried. (as cited in DeWitt, 2020)

Ongoing stress affects the way people think, which affects their ability to feel peace and equanimity. Meditation teacher Hugh Poulton compiled a questionnaire, which revealed a list of common thoughts that enter people's minds when they are stressed and feeling frantic, including (as cited in Williams & Penman, 2011, pp. 140–141):

- I can't enjoy myself without thinking about what needs to be done.
- I must never fail.
- Why can't I relax?
- It's up to me.
- I must be strong.
- Everyone relies on me.
- I'm the only one who can do this.
- I can't stand this anymore.
- I mustn't waste a minute.
- I wish I were somewhere else.
- Why don't they just do it?
- Why am I not enjoying this anymore?
- What's the matter with me?
- I can't give up.
- Something has to change.
- There must be something wrong with me.
- Everything will fall apart without me.
- Why can't I switch off?

Have you ever had one or more of these thoughts? Although normal, these thoughts are symptoms of ongoing stress. Through mindfulness practice, you can learn to witness these thoughts and let them go. You can learn to be more self-aware of your own ingrained thought patterns, letting go of those that no longer serve you or managing your reactions to them. Mindfulness can change your response to stress by bringing awareness to what troubles you, as well as helping you interpret and respond more effectively. As poet, playwright, and actor William Shakespeare (2016/1599) wrote in *Hamlet*, "There is nothing either good or bad but thinking makes it so."

Improved Emotional Intelligence

Another benefit of mindfulness particular to school leaders is improved emotional intelligence. *Emotional intelligence* is the ability to recognize your own emotions with intelligence, as well as understand, manage, and influence the emotions of others (Mayer, Caruso, & Salovey, 2016). High levels of emotional intelligence allow leaders to intentionally manage their thoughts and feelings as opposed to operating automatically. Further, emotionally intelligent school leaders are better able to understand the thoughts and feelings of others. Daniel Goleman (1995; as cited in Iberlin, 2017, pp. 7–8), author, psychologist, and science journalist, described *emotional intelligence* as having these emotional and social competencies:

1. **Self-awareness:** This type of mindfulness means being aware of what one feels and using this understanding to make decisions. With self-awareness, practitioners have the ability to differentiate between subtleties in feelings such as recognizing when they are self-conscious, anxious, overly tired, irritable, or depressed.

2. **Self-regulation:** When people are mindful of their feelings, they can consider how to control their emotions so that they add to their well-being. For example, if people are irritable, self-regulation can give them the ability to recognize they are working in a less-than-optimal state so that they can take steps to change their state or situation. One way a person could combat stress, for instance, would be to employ deep breathing exercises.

3. **Self-motivation:** This state of mindfulness enables people to set goals, have the persistence to take steps toward their goals, and eventually achieve their goals.

4. **Empathy**: This is defined as understanding how others are feeling and having rapport with diverse groups of people.

5. **Social skills:** These skills allow individuals to feel comfortable in social situations and to interact smoothly. It includes having strong people skills and knowing how to interpret the actions of others.

Emotionally intelligent school leaders recognize the triggers in themselves and others, so they are more capable of handling highly charged, emotional situations. *Mindful emotional intelligence* is bringing your whole mind (emotional intelligence) and whole heart (mindfulness) to your leadership practice (Six Seconds, 2021; see figure 1.1).

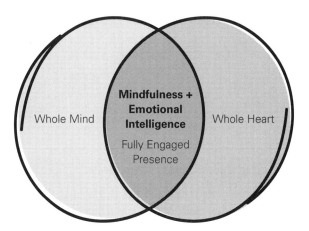

Source: Adapted from SixSeconds, 2021.

FIGURE 1.1: Mindful emotional intelligence involves the whole mind and heart.

Improved Social Relationships

Improved social relationships is yet another benefit of mindfulness helpful to school leaders. Relationships are critical to nearly all aspects of effective school leadership and to a high-functioning organization (Duffy, Ganster, & Pagon, 2002). Without authentic and trusting relationships, it is difficult for school leaders to bring staff and parents together toward common goals and a clear vision to improve student achievement and well-being. What results is a low-trust, low-commitment environment. Mindfulness increases positive interpersonal relationships by increasing your ability to understand other perspectives and reducing knee-jerk, habitual reactions (Giluk, 2010). This is especially true in schools, where leaders need to reach out to the varied stakeholders including students, parents, teachers, support staff, and community members.

The numerous benefits of mindfulness to school leaders also extend to the demanding and broad expectations of school leadership. In his book *Leading in a Culture of Change*, award-winning author Michael Fullan (2020) emphasizes that successful leaders need energy, enthusiasm, and hope. Fullan (2020) sees the principal's role as having a clear moral purpose: developing relationships, building knowledge, and striving for coherence in a nonlinear world. James M. Kouzes, executive fellow, and Barry Z. Posner (2010), chair and professor, both in the Leavey School of Business at Santa Clara University, view leadership as "an affair of the heart," adding, "Leaders are in love with their constituents, their customers and clients, and the mission that they are serving" (pp. 136, xxiv).

A meta-analysis by leadership experts Robert J. Marzano and Timothy Waters (2009) found leaders responsible for collaborative goal setting, establishing non-negotiable goals for achievement and instruction, monitoring said goals, and advocating resources to support the goals. Based on research and field studies, the Wallace Foundation (2013) highlighted the following five key practices essential for principals.

1. **Shape a vision.** Effective school principals help establish a norm of high expectations for all students. This motivates everyone to work toward a common goal. It is the school leader's role to build intentionality toward the school's vision.

2. **Create a hospitable climate.** A healthy environment for learning not only requires orderliness and safety but also immense support, respect, and responsiveness toward all. When a school climate is healthy, there is trust and collaboration among all stakeholders. The school leader builds and models these attributes through fostering strong relationships and shared leadership.

3. **Cultivate leadership in others.** Effective school leaders provide stakeholders opportunities to influence decision making. They help establish a professional community where teachers work together toward improving instruction. This includes a focus on clearly defined and well-articulated standards of learning for all students.

4. **Improve instruction.** By maintaining a strong focus on quality instruction and professional learning, school leaders can improve classroom instruction. Through formal and informal observations of classrooms (focused on learning and professional growth), leaders can impact the quality of instruction on a daily basis. At the core of improved instruction is maintaining the belief that all teachers can learn, grow, and improve.

5. **Manage people, data, and processes to foster school improvement.** Effective school leaders use data to identify problems and understand the causes. They build collaboration on rigorous goals and offer support to both students and staff to meet the goals. They challenge low expectations by revisiting the vision of high expectations for all.

To strive toward these broad and demanding expectations, principals would benefit in the practice of mindful leadership.

Summary

This chapter discussed the definitions of *mindfulness* and *mindful leadership* and provided an overview of the history of mindfulness and its acceptance in 21st century society. It presented the neuroscientific information relating to mindfulness and the benefits of mindfulness in the workplace. It also discussed the attitudes that support mindful school leaders and provided examples of these attitudes in the workplace.

The next chapter discusses the importance of beginning mindfulness practices within oneself. It includes many mindfulness tools from meditation to self-compassion, providing a solid base to use as a springboard for utilizing mindfulness practices toward others.

Reflection Questions

Take a moment to respond to the following reflection questions, either in thought or in writing, before moving on to the next chapter.

1. What is my definition of *mindfulness*?

2. How would I define *mindful leadership*?

3. How can mindful leadership improve my role as a school leader?

4. In what ways am I already showing up as a mindful school leader?

CHAPTER 2

Beginning Within

To lead others, you must first lead yourself.

—Raymond M. Kethledge and Michael S. Erwin

Mindfulness practice begins within yourself. By first focusing on developing mindfulness practices within yourself, you will strengthen your self-awareness and self-regulation (Mager, 2019). As a result, you will notice whether your mind and heart remain open during stressful and challenging interactions. However, if you find your immediate responses to such interactions are physical symptoms of anger or stress (for example, a racing heart or clenched fists), or if you immediately jump to negative thoughts or assumptions that then hamper your work, you will likely benefit from mindfulness practices designed to initially affect only you.

Over time, mindfulness practice brings feelings of quiet contentment, a sense of peaceful well-being, and a "combination of aliveness and centeredness" (Hanson, 2009, p. 59). Through your mindfulness practice, you will learn what truly matters to you in your personal and work lives. It is important for you, as a leader, to focus on your deepest priorities because numerous needs vie for your attention. Without mindfulness, you may feel pressure to multitask, doing everything at once and nothing well. Being a healthy, caring, compassionate leader is both challenging and possible, thus benefiting students, staff, parents, and community through your centeredness and presence.

Buddhist monk Thich Nhat Hanh said, "The longest journey you will ever take is the eighteen inches from your head to your heart" (as cited in Diwanji, 2019). As a good leader, you may have a strong IQ, but to be a *great* leader, you must strengthen the qualities of your heart. These include self-compassion, compassion for others, empathy, self-awareness, and a state of being present in the here and now.

This chapter introduces nine formal mindfulness tools to help you begin within and, over time, build a foundation of compassion, peacefulness, awareness, and centeredness. For each tool, I provide an overview of the research and the benefits, plus step-by-step instructions on how to perform each practice. At the end of the chapter, you will have an opportunity to reflect on these tools and consider your personal readiness for beginning each practice.

Nine Mindfulness Tools for Beginning Within

If you are new to mindfulness, scan the mindful activities in this chapter and choose one to begin with. It may be most beneficial to begin with mindful breathing, since the breath serves as a foundation of mindfulness (Halliwell, 2020). Once you are comfortable with a practice, experiment with another, and so on. If you are already an experienced mindfulness practitioner, you may choose to incorporate more of the practices. Ultimately, you will use the nine-week mindfulness implementation plan in chapter 4 (page 87) as a reference when you are ready to begin implementing these tools in your personal and professional lives. Although these nine mindfulness tools are practices that benefit you personally at first, later you will see how the skills transfer naturally to the school setting.

Mindful Breathing

As a school leader, you will find it is incredibly valuable to have easy-to-use mindfulness tools at hand that do not take a lot of time, yet provide a sense of peace, stillness, and happiness. Practices that focus on the breath are perhaps the easiest place to begin. Mindfulness training encourages you to pause, breathe, and subsequently respond more effectively to your experiences. Your breath is your life source. It is an anchor in mindfulness practices. The well-known Zen monk, Thich Nhat Hanh (2015), described mindful breathing in this way:

> We follow our in-breath and our out-breath, making space for silence. We say to ourselves, "Breathing in, I know I'm breathing in."

Breathing in and out mindfully, paying attention only to the breath, we can quiet all the noise within us—the chattering about the past, the future, and the longing for something more. (p. 5)

Different types of breathing provide different results. Focusing on the breath can slow the heart rate, relax the body, increase clarity, and improve happiness (Catherine, 2008). This practice is both calming and invigorating, helping you stay grounded, even during intense situations.

You can utilize mindful breathing anytime, anywhere. You take nearly twenty thousand breaths each day, and you can train yourself to be conscious of your breathing. Noticing the natural rhythm of your breathing is a powerful mindfulness practice. Not only does breathing provide oxygen to your physical body but also the ability to calm and soothe your mind and emotions (Halliwell, 2020). You can ease stressful situations by taking the time to focus on your breath.

Two specific breathing activities—(1) belly breathing, and (2) box breathing—are excellent mindfulness practices for leaders to implement anytime. I recommend you practice these activities a few times in a quiet space (beginning within) before implementing them in the school setting.

BELLY BREATHING

Belly breathing is an easy and completely natural mindfulness tool; even babies and puppies can do it! With belly breathing, you take deep, conscious breaths beginning with inhaling through the nose and then exhaling through the nose while focusing on the rise and fall of your belly. It's this rise and fall of your belly that lets you know you are doing it correctly. Belly breathing, also referred to as *diaphragmatic breathing*, is one of the easiest ways to bring about relaxation (Duke Human Resources, n.d.). It is important to be present during the sensations of breathing in and out. The steps of belly breathing are as follows.

1. Sit in a comfortable position or lie down. Allow the belly to relax and soften by simply noticing if you are holding your belly in. Place your hand on your belly so that you will be able to feel your breathing.

2. As you breathe in through your nose, feel your belly expand. It might help to imagine a balloon being inflated. As you breathe out, feel your belly contract. The balloon deflates. This is one belly breath.

3. Repeat four or more times.

Belly breathing allows you to relax. It signals to your brain that it is OK to feel ease. This activity takes only one to two minutes (depending on how many breaths you take) and serves as a powerful reset. I recommend you come back to belly breathing anytime you feel irritation, anxiety, or stress. Even one focused belly breath is beneficial.

Imagine you are about to present your school's data and related professional development plan to the board of trustees. You have prepared well, organizing your presentation and anticipating answers to potential questions. In spite of your immense preparation, you can feel your heart racing. Your thoughts are spinning with self-doubt. To calm yourself, you bring your attention to your belly. You allow it to soften. Consciously, you breathe in through your nose and feel your belly expand. As you breathe out, you notice it contract. For a minute or two, you repeat this focus on the in- and out-breath, and the soft rising and falling of your abdomen. Calmness starts to seep in. You are now in a much better place to make your presentation.

BOX BREATHING

Box breathing is a simple exercise that uses a box or square shape as a visual cue to help practice mindful breathing. It is referred to as *box breathing* because a box has four sides. The breathing pattern is based on four parts—inhale, hold, exhale, hold. Doing this exercise helps you learn to breathe naturally from your diaphragm. Former U.S. Navy SEAL Commander Mark Divine began training Navy SEALs in this breathing technique after using it while in active duty:

> Box breathing is a technique that helps you take control of your automatic breathing patterns to train your breath for optimal health and performance. . . . It combines the practice of optimal breathing with parasympathetic activation, concentration and mindfulness training. (as cited in Nazish, 2019)

Box breathing involves the following six steps, as illustrated in figure 2.1.

1. Sit comfortably in a chair or on the floor.
2. Look for a box or rectangle shape, such as a window or picture frame, to use as your visual cue.
3. Start at the upper-left corner of the box shape and inhale through your nose for a count of four as you move your eyes along the top of the box.

4. As you move down the right side of the box, hold your breath for another count of four.

5. As you move along the bottom of the box, exhale for the same count.

6. As you move your eyes up the left side of the box, hold your breath and count to four again.

7. Repeat steps 1–6 four more times.

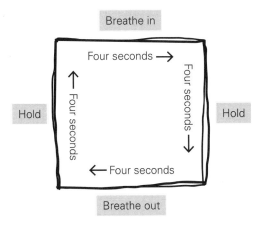

FIGURE 2.1: Box breathing diagram.

For people not accustomed to holding their breath, holding their breath four counts can cause anxiety. If this happens to you, it is fine to shorten the breathing time to two or three counts. This activity takes only a few minutes, but yields great results in restoring a sense of calmness and aliveness. Divine valued this practice so much he credits it with saving his life: "It was instrumental in saving my life several times in crises. I was able to remain calm and focus clearly to avoid reactionary thinking, or, worse, panic" (as cited in Nazish, 2019). As a school leader, you may not find your life at risk, but you're certainly no stranger to crisis. This technique is likely to bring you the same ability to remain calm and avoid reactionary thinking as you manage times of stress.

Mark Gordon, a former school board member in the district in which I had worked and governor of Wyoming, finds box breathing a valuable tool. After I taught it to him while he was in the throes of running for governor, Gordon shared with me that of all the tools and advice people had offered him, he found box breathing to be the most valuable. Anywhere he looked, there was a picture, a door, or a window to help him visualize his 4-4-4-4 breathing. It helped him remain calm under the barrage of questioning that happens in any political arena (M. Gordon, personal communication, January 1, 2021).

Intentional Silence

School and district leaders routinely find themselves in positions of speaking and listening. Since these are natural and inherent aspects of leadership, they make the need for leaders to experience silence all the more important. *Intentional silence* means purposefully being silent for a given period of time, providing an opportunity to disconnect from the busy, stressful life of a school leader and give a break to the parts of your brain involved in speaking and listening. Taking time for quiet moments helps improve overall well-being and alleviate stress (Goldstein, 2007). This intentional silence gives your brain time to just *be*. According to Krishna Bhatta, a urologist and founder of the meditation app Relax, "Just like when your body is continually working, your brain gets tired. If you don't take breaks, it will become exhausted" (as cited in Laurence, 2020). This can cause edginess or anxiety (Laurence, 2020). A 2020 study revealed silence can elevate positive moods and increase relaxation. These findings show that silence can actually promote well-being (Pfeifer & Wittmann, 2020).

Through intentional silence:

> People are more able to notice the subtlest of sounds—birdsong, a child's laughter, the honking of a horn in the distance, or the sound of a mindfulness chime. Each one of these sounds, when given one's attention, can serve as reminders to listen mindfully, to be aware, to be present, to notice. (Iberlin, 2017, p. 24)

According to clinical psychologist Chloe Carmichael (2021), two areas of the brain need a break from the noise of everyday life: (1) *Wernicke's area*, which is responsible for listening, and (2) *Broca's area*, which is responsible for speech. This much-needed break allows people to communicate more effectively. People learn to pause, think, and then speak as opposed to immediately responding to input via verbal or written methods. Intermittent silence can also make you more aware of the words you choose to use when you do speak. Carmichael (2021) compares it to *intermittent fasting*, when people become more aware of the food they are ingesting after taking a break from eating. For school leaders, who are constantly interacting either in writing or verbally, it is important to be aware that silence can indeed be golden.

Further, a 2015 study revealed that silence actually stimulates growth of new neurons in the hippocampus (Kirste, Nicola, Kronenberg, Walker, Liu, & Kempermann, 2015). Although the research is preliminary, neuron growth matters to people's brains. Depression and dementia are linked to the decrease of neurons in the hippocampus (Kirste et al., 2015).

The four steps to intentional silence are as follows.

1. In a quiet area, set a timer for ten minutes. Feel free to adjust this time as appropriate for your schedule.
2. Close your mouth to avoid talking.
3. Close your eyes.
4. Observe your thoughts; for example, notice if you are rehearsing for an upcoming meeting or rehashing an interaction you had with a parent. Simply watch each thought come and go, like clouds passing in the sky.

You can practice intentional silence anytime, but it can be especially useful prior to the beginning of an anticipated stressful workday. Bhatta (2019), a surgeon at Northern Light Health, encourages the practice of intermittent silence to prevent burnout and replenish lost energy. Bhatta (2019) recommends taking short breaks of intermittent silence when feelings of stress or anger begin to arise. He also recommends ten minutes a day to garner energy and improve one's outlook on life.

Since people begin learning to observe and communicate (verbally and nonverbally) practically from the moment they're born, the practice of intentional silence will not seem natural at first. If you suffer from depression, anxiety, or other mental health conditions, intermittent silence may be especially difficult. As you drop into silence, your inner negative voices and spinning thoughts may seem louder, according to Jamie Price, creator of the wellness and mindfulness app MyLife (as cited in Yuko, 2020). Price also noted that some people feel a low-level hum of anxiety during silence (as cited in Yuko, 2020). If you find intermittent silence too trying, feel free to shorten the amount of time or abandon the practice and try other mindfulness activities. Alternatively, you could begin with small acts of silence, such as driving without music playing, going for a walk or run without your headphones, or making dinner without the background distraction of the television.

Although intentional silence seems like a solitary practice, you can also practice it alongside a spouse, colleague, student, or friend. Celebrating the gift of silence together can be both rejuvenating and calming. You may want to spend time afterward discussing the experience of silence. As you become accustomed to intentional silence, you will gradually find peace and calmness.

The following fictional scenario illustrates one manner of incorporating intentional silence into your life.

Dominic is an elementary principal. His day is rife with noises, conversations, meetings, written communications, and varied conflicts. As the day ends, he is eager to be with his own family at home, which is also filled with different types of noises, conversations, and conflicts. When he nears his home, Dominic stops just two blocks short at a nearby park. He pulls into a secluded area and sets his smartphone to alert him after ten minutes. Then, he sits. He allows his eyes to gently close. The numerous interactions of his day and plans for tomorrow flood his mind at first. He watches each thought come and go, unattached. He can feel himself relax. When the timer chimes, alerting him the ten minutes is up, he starts his car and finishes his commute home. This ten-minute routine has become a ritual for Dominic. He finds that it helps put his day behind him, leaving him better able to attend to his wife and children's needs.

Mindful Meditation

As a school leader, being mindful gives you the experience of sitting still and feeling how mindfulness can open your heart and calm your mind. Instead of constantly focusing on being a results-driven, high-achieving, ambitious leader, you learn to turn your focus within, and a subtle transformation begins. Often, your accomplishments as a leader do not increase your peace of mind. *Mindful meditation* is training yourself to be more aware of both your inner world and what is happening in the moment. It offers numerous benefits for you personally and as a leader.

Research shows that meditation is a powerful practice for improving psychological well-being and overall mood (Bostock, Crosswell, Prather, & Steptoe, 2019; Broderick, 2005), decreasing anxiety (Hofmann, Sawyer, Witt, & Oh, 2010; Orme-Johnson & Barnes, 2014; Rod, 2015), enhancing job satisfaction (Bostock et al., 2019; Hülsheger et al., 2013), decreasing depression (Rod, 2015), and increasing positive emotions (Geschwind, Peeters, Drukker, van Os, & Wichers, 2011).

There are numerous types of meditation, all sharing the goal of bringing a sense of calmness, peace, and relaxation (see Mayo Clinic Staff, 2022a).

- **Mindful meditation.** In mindful meditation, bring your attention to the present moment. Observe your thoughts and gently let them go without judging your thinking. Focus on the present-moment experience, on the in-and-out flow of your breath.

- **Guided meditation.** Formulate images of places or situations you find relaxing, while engaging many of your senses.

- **Mantra meditation.** Silently repeat a word or phrase, such as *om,* to help keep you focused.

- **Transcendental meditation.** Repeat a personal mantra in a specific manner.

According to senior neurologist and clinical psychologist Rick Hanson (2009), "Mindfulness leads to wisdom, and the best way to increase mindfulness is meditation" (p. 203). *Meditation* allows you to be with your mind fully, growing inner strengths, including "calm and insight that enable you to feel all your feelings and face your shadows even when it's hard" (Hanson, 2013, p. 8). In my own experience, mindful meditation also provides me with similar benefits as intentional silence (page 40) in terms of gaining a sense of peace from having time to myself.

Creating a regular pattern of mindful meditation can prove difficult at first because the benefits may not be readily apparent. Contemplating the benefits of meditation may help you develop a regular, disciplined meditative practice. Knowing its benefits are research-based can help you prioritize time for this valuable practice.

Before engaging in a meditation practice, it is important to understand the following (Iberlin, 2017, p. 37).

> Meditation can be surprisingly difficult. The process itself is simple, but it is not easy to do successfully. It requires lots of practice, and people often have a hard time with it at first.
>
> It's okay to start with short meditations at first—even five minutes or less is both challenging and beneficial.
>
> If thoughts interrupt one's meditation and focus on breathing, notice the thoughts but let them go and return the focus to breathing.
>
> Deep breathing is from the diaphragm (muscles in the torso that expand and contract the lungs). The inhale should cause the abdomen or stomach area to expand. The exhale should cause the abdomen to contract. The chest moves very little during this type of breathing.
>
> Meditation has the most benefits when one practices it consistently over time.

The following eight steps will guide you in beginning a mindful meditation practice.

1. Begin by sitting comfortably on the floor in a cross-legged position or upright in a chair with your feet on the ground. You may want to lean against the back of a chair or wall to support your back. Aim for a comfortable position—the space between slouching and rigid. Set your hands palms down on your thighs, or hold them palms up in a gesture of openness. If you like, allow your index fingers and thumbs to lightly touch, a traditional meditation posture called *gyan mudra* (see figure 2.2).

FIGURE 2.2: The gyan mudra.

   Although the mind is more attentive while in a seated position, it is also fine to meditate while lying down, but be aware that the mind often associates lying down with sleeping (Stibich, 2020). To do this, lie on your back with your legs hip-width apart. Allow your arms to lie comfortably by your side with your palms up.

2. Use a chime, bell, or timer to begin your session. Set the timer for five to ten minutes, or longer for experienced meditators. I recommend the free Insight Timer app (https://insighttimer.com) for this purpose. Not only does this app let you set a duration, but it also tracks the number of consecutive days you meditate, which can add an extra layer of motivation to be consistent in your meditation practice. You can find other suggestions for timers and guided meditations in the appendix, page 101, which offers myriad helpful resources.

3. Close your eyes if you feel comfortable doing so. If not, focus your eyes on a spot on the ground about six feet away. Take several comfortable breaths in and out through your nose while focusing on your breath.

4. Relax your shoulders, jaw, eyes, and forehead.

5. Continue to breathe in and out slowly while focusing on your breath. You may want to notice the gentle rise and fall of your belly or the feeling of taking in air through your nostrils.

6. Thoughts will arise as you sit. Gently watch them come and go. See your thoughts as clouds passing in the sky or as bubbles rising up and popping. Welcome yourself back to your breath in a gentle manner.

7. Continue this cycle for five to ten minutes or longer. When the chime or bell ends your meditation session, gently open your eyes.

8. Allow yourself time to transition slowly back to the pace of your life. If time allows, sit for a few moments longer. If your mind begins to immediately revert to your to-do list, remind yourself that you'll come back to it soon.

Mindful meditation, over time, leads you to feel more positivity and peacefulness, and gain an improved attention span (Cassata, 2021). Because it takes time to reap the numerous results, mindful meditation is a practice, something you must do consistently to achieve its benefits. I liken it to lifting weights; with continued practice, you build muscle. If you stop lifting weights, you lose the benefits. Mindful practitioners often bookend their meditation time, choosing to either begin or end their day with the practice. This is because they often have more control over how their days begin and end than they do over their time while at work. As you begin developing your mindfulness habits, aim for the same time and location each day.

If you are new to meditation, it may be helpful to know that spending just thirteen minutes a day for a period of eight weeks enhances attention, memory, mood, and self-regulation (Basso, McHale, Ende, Oberlin, & Suzuki, 2019). The same study found these benefits did not convey from just four weeks of meditation. So, if you find thirteen minutes or longer difficult to commit to, I recommended you begin with an amount of time that does seem achievable for daily practice—for example, five minutes—and then gradually increase it to at least thirteen minutes to reap the benefits.

What's most important about mindful meditation is that it's less about that amount of time than it is about your commitment to the process. Kabat-Zinn (1994) puts it this way:

> It is important to know that meditation has little to do with clock time. Five minutes of formal practice can be profound or more so than forty-five minutes. The sincerity of your effort matters far more than elapsed time, since we are really talking about stepping out of minutes and hours and into moments. (p. 123)

Whatever amount of time you choose for your meditation practice, it is important to practice consistently.

The following fictional scenario depicts one strategy that has proved successful for many mindfulness meditators.

Christine, a high school principal busy with a toddler, baby, and spouse, links her mindful meditation to brushing her teeth. Since she brushes twice daily, it is easy for her to remember her meditation practice. Before she brushes in the morning, Christine meditates for eight minutes. Again in the evening before brushing her teeth, she meditates another eight minutes. Breaking her meditation time into two chunks makes it more manageable with her frantic schedule.

Daily Intention Setting

Being pulled in different directions each work day is an all-too-common reality for school leaders. From handling discipline issues to rehearsing safety drills, school leadership is taxing. In the midst of your constant *doing*, daily intention setting helps create a sense of *being*.

Daily intention setting is a practice that improves self-awareness and motivation, while helping leaders focus on what is important. An *intention* describes your dreams as an action step. It serves as a compass, guiding you to align with how you want to appear in your career and personal lives. It is a positive statement about something you'd like to attain. Writer and personal growth expert Omar Itani (2010) states:

> In Yogic philosophy, an intention is referred to as a *Sankalpa*. This term comes from the Sanskrit roots *san*, meaning "a connection with the highest truth," and *Kalpa*, meaning "vow." An intention, or Sankalpa, then, is a solemn vow and commitment we make with ourselves to support our highest truth.

Intention setting helps you be mindful of what matters, giving less attention to the myriad distractions of being a school leader. Melissa Maxx, a certified mindfulness coach writes of intention setting, "Instead of feeling like a victim of circumstance, you become the conscious creator of your days and your life" (as cited in Houlis, 2021). For example, a principal who has an upcoming meeting with a typically hostile parent might set the intention, *Today my intention is to stay calm and centered in whatever arises for the benefit of those I serve and for my own well-being.*

Setting intentions each day is different from goal setting. A goal might be to read an educational journal article each week. An intention would be to read educational journals to gain knowledge about best educational practices. *Intentions*, in other words, clarify your purpose and underlying values. Intention setting takes just a few minutes each day, ideally in the morning before beginning your workday.

The following four steps will guide you in mindfully setting your daily intentions.

1. Reflect for a few minutes about what attitude would be beneficial for your day. Think about what would make your day more meaningful.

2. Write your intention as a positive statement using *I will* rather than *I won't*. For example, an intention for your workday could be worded, *Today, I will be present for staff, students, and parents*. You might consider writing your intention on a sticky note and placing it on your computer for easy reference.

3. Ensure your intentions are actionable for a typical workday. For example, you could intend, *I will connect with teachers during today's staff meeting, taking time to listen to their concerns*.

4. At the end of the day, reflect on how you upheld your intentions. Do this with compassion toward yourself. Intentions are commitments to yourself, and you should not judge yourself harshly. Take time to reflect on how you could improve in similar situations in the future.

Living with intention helps you connect to the present moment. It empowers you by aligning both your thoughts and actions with the qualities you wish to embody. In just a few minutes a day, you can mindfully align your purpose and values.

The following fictional scenario depicts an example of a school leader setting an intention for the day.

With his coffee in hand, Jim, a junior high principal, pauses to consider what he wants for this day. He thinks about where he needs to put his focus to lead and live meaningfully. He thinks about what attitude he wants to model for his staff and students. Since he's been away attending numerous meetings throughout the week, Jim jots his intention on a sticky note: *Today I intend to authentically connect with students and staff by giving them my time and full attention.*

Jim takes a moment to reflect on how this intention fits into his larger values. When he arrives at his office, he places the sticky note on his computer screen to serve as a reminder. Jim also sets an alarm on his phone to chime at 10:00 a.m., noon, and 2:00 p.m. so he can briefly pause and reflect on whether he is living up to his intention.

Unplugging

Technology, social media, and other innovations have made a school leader's life much easier in some ways. Cell phones have made it easier for administrative assistants, educators, and parents to be in touch with school leaders. Email has made written communication quicker. Social media has proven to be a great avenue for communicating with parents. However, the nonstop use of these tools can truly impact the quality of your life and relationships with others.

Think of *unplugging* as intentionally and completely taking a break from all technology, including smartphones, the internet, and other digital devices. Technology in and of itself is not bad; however, constant attention to and reliance on technology can affect your ability to focus and sustain attention on the task at hand (Christakis, 2011).

Further, studies have shown that when cell phones are present (whether or not they are actually in use) people feel less connected, and the mere presence of a cell phone negatively affects the quality of conversation. This is especially true when the discussion pertains to personally meaningful topics (Przybylski & Weinstein, 2013). People are so dependent on technology that on average, they check their cell phones every 6.5 minutes (Spencer, 2013). According to the PEW Research Center, 47 percent of smartphone users rarely turn off their phones, and another 36 percent never do (Rainie & Zickuhr, 2015). In fact, according to a Nielsen (2016) report, the average person is connected to technology nearly eleven hours a day. The consequences of people's attention to technology includes lower emotional intelligence, motivation, social skills, and empathy, and increased interpersonal conflicts (Scott, Valley, & Simecka, 2017).

School leaders often use social media to reach out to stakeholders. Facebook and Twitter, for example, are avenues to communicate about upcoming parent-teacher conferences, field trips, and other events. Leaders can share information in real time, including during sporting events and school board meetings. However, it is important to not remain constantly connected to social media because certain negative emotions are linked to its overuse.

In a study at the University of Pennsylvania, researchers found that one group limiting social media to thirty minutes per day significantly reduced depression and loneliness compared to the control group (Hunt, Marx, Lipson, & Young, 2018). These findings suggest that limiting social media can lead to improvements in overall well-being (Hunt et al., 2018). Unplugging also provides a break from the negative emotions connected to social media. Powering down will give you more opportunities to have mindful moments throughout your day.

Dana Bender (n.d.), a wellness strategy manager and National Board Certified Health and Wellness Coach, offers these questions to assist you in cultivating mindful breaks from technology:

1. Are you taking time to pay attention to your internal state (energy, mood, stress) throughout the week following high technology use?
2. If yes, how do you notice when you need to detach from technology and reset? What happens in your body and/or mind when this occurs?
3. If not, when and where could you start incorporating this mindful check during your week?

Although it is difficult for school leaders to unplug from technology at school, the following four steps will provide more time to socialize with employees, students, family, and friends in face-to-face conversations.

1. Set a personal goal for limiting technology in the workplace. Due to the on-call demand of school leadership, this could be as simple as having no cell phone visible during face-to-face interactions.
2. Set a personal or family goal for reducing technology use at home. Create technology-free times, such as during meals.
3. Set a personal or family goal for creating technology-free spaces. This may include the bedroom or dining room.
4. Create a habit of *not* checking your smartphone first thing in the morning. Instead, begin your day with mindfulness practices such as intention setting (page 46) and meditation (page 42).

Taking the steps to unplug periodically provides more time and mindfulness in your day. It also builds emotional fluency through improved face-to-face interactions. Even short breaks from technology will leave you feeling more energized and refreshed. Over time, unplugging from technology will become a natural part of your mindfulness practices.

The following fictional scenario describes a school leader making a conscious effort to unplug for parts of her day.

Candace, an intermediate school principal, found herself obsessively checking Facebook posts related to her school. Also, she was never without her cell phone, constantly checking emails, phone calls, and text messages. The first thing Candace did every morning was grab her cell phone and begin reading new posts or recent text messages. Upon reflecting on her ongoing use of technology, she realized it was having an adverse effect on her by causing feelings of anxiousness. Candace decided to set some personal boundaries for her use of technology. She made a goal to begin each day with a brief meditation before reading the latest posts and texts. She also began to put her cell phone in a desk drawer prior to any meetings. Her final change was to ban cell phones from the dinner table. After a few weeks, Candace noticed feeling less anxious in relation to her nearly constant use of technology.

Mindful Pauses

There are a whirlwind of constant noises, interruptions, and chaos in the life of a school leader. Indeed, the pace of school leadership can leave you feeling disconnected from your personal vision of success. Engaging in *mindful pauses*, regular moments to slow down and check in with your emotions and feelings, not only empowers you to respond to events rather than react, but also gives you opportunities to refresh and energize. Jack Kornfield (2009), an American author and trained Buddhist monk, described the benefits of pausing this way:

> In a moment of stopping, we break the spell between past results and automatic reaction. When we pause, we can notice the actual experience, the pain or pleasure, fear or excitement. In the stillness before our habits arise, we become free to act wisely. (p. 97)

Best-selling author and CEO of The Energy Project, Tony Schwartz (2010) expresses similar sentiments: "Human beings perform best and are most productive when they alternate between periods of intense focus and intermittent renewal."

Mindful pauses take little time; you can accomplish them in just thirty seconds. You can systematically build mindful pauses into your day by allocating time (for example, before getting out of bed, prior to commuting to work, at midday, and just before retiring for the evening). A mindful pause can take many forms. It can be as simple as stopping what you are doing and taking three slow breaths while being aware of the present moment. You might focus on a mantra of breathing in peace and breathing out any tension or stress you feel.

The following are two mindful pause practices. I adapted the first from mindful author and podcast host Cara Bradley (2018). The second is based on the acronym *STOP*.

MINDFUL PAUSE PRACTICE

1. Sit comfortably in a chair with your feet on the floor. Place your hands on your thighs. If you feel comfortable doing so, close your eyes. If not, just gaze at the floor about six feet in front of you.

2. Notice your feet on the ground, notice your seat in the chair, and notice your hands on your lap.

3. Bring your attention to your heart beating by finding your pulse.

4. Place attention on the rhythm of your breathing. With your mind noticing your inhalations and exhalations, you may start to notice a sense of relaxation.

5. For the next few moments, choose to place your attention on your feet, hands, heart rate, or breath. Simply notice. Then ask yourself, "Which of my character strengths are needed in this moment?"

6. Open your eyes (if they have been closed). Take a moment to be aware of what the pause did for you. Your body is a stabilizing system when you take the opportunity to balance.

The mindful pause provides a much-needed moment of silence in your busy life. Taking time to balance your nervous system and enjoy a sense of peacefulness helps you become less reactive. Calling on your character strengths helps you be more intentional, as the following fictional scenario shows.

Stefan, a high school athletic director, was about to meet with a set of aggressive parents. Previously, the parents had showed tremendous hostility toward the basketball coach for not giving their daughter enough playing time. Although his schedule was incredibly busy, Stefan took a moment for a mindful pause just prior to his upcoming meeting. He closed his office door and sat in a chair facing the window and paid close attention to his heart rate and breathing. He simply sat for forty-five seconds. Then Stefan asked himself, "Which of my strengths is needed now?" The word *empathy* came immediately to his mind. He knew being defensive or aggressive with the parents wouldn't help. Stefan planned to try to put himself in their shoes, while still supporting the school's basketball coach.

STOP PRACTICE

Stress is a normal part of being alive. In and of itself, stress is not the problem. However, the way people react to stress can cause additional stress. Over time, if your reactions are not normalized, pent-up stress can lead to changes in mood, muscle tension, and anxiety (Scott, 2022). Research reveals that four of five principals often experience job-related stress (Jones, 2022). Similar to mindful pauses, the *STOP practice* helps leaders ease a worried mind and find equilibrium. It helps strengthen your level of self-awareness. Further, like the previously mentioned mindful pause practice (page 51), you can accomplish it in less than a minute or two.

The STOP practice has four basic steps, following the acronym *STOP*.

1. The *S* is for *stopping* what you are doing in the moment to take a minute to pause.

2. The *T* is a reminder about *taking* in a few deep, cleansing breaths through your nose. You may notice your breathing is shallow. It may help to place your hand on your belly to encourage breathing from the diaphragm. Notice how your belly expands and contracts with each breath.

3. The *O* is for *observing* your thoughts and feelings. Just the act of noticing can have a calming effect on the body. There is no need to fix anything; just observe. Simply acknowledge your thoughts and feelings, allowing space for them to just be as they are.

4. The *P* is for *proceeding* with your day with awareness and gentleness.

Try not to worry whether or not you're doing it right. STOP is designed to be a short practice to help you center yourself. Christiane Wolf, a physician-turned-mindfulness teacher, and J. Greg Serpa (2015), clinical psychologist, offer this advice:

> Sometimes, you may notice that the sensations in the body, your thoughts, or your emotions have changed, and sometimes you might notice that they haven't changed at all. You are still doing it just right. The goal is to notice, not to change your experience. (p. 128)

Think of the STOP practice as a time-out to re-center and re-energize. By being mindfully aware of your breath, you will be able to return to a state of balance and ease. It can help you shift from automatic responses to being more intentional. Consider various times of the day when you can add both mindful pauses and the STOP practice, as the principal in the following fictional scenario does.

Chad, a high school principal, happened to pass by the teachers' lounge. Ruth, one of the English teachers, was repeating very inappropriate gossip she had heard in her classroom. Chad could feel his temper rising. His first instinct was to march into the lounge and lash out at Ruth. Instead, he reminded himself to pause. Chad then went through the four steps of the STOP practice. He noticed his heart was still racing, but his thoughts were more composed. He entered the lounge and asked what was up. From a more composed place, Chad reminded the staff members present about students' rights to confidentiality. He made a mental note to talk to Ruth one-on-one at a later time.

Self-Compassion

Often, it is difficult to navigate the pressures and demands of school leadership. High achievers often have tendencies toward perfectionism. When things go wrong in the workplace (and they invariably will), leaders tend to focus on self-blame and self-criticism. The goal is not to deny failures or setbacks but to contextualize them productively and use them to improve. To offset these self-deprecating feelings, *self-compassion* offers a valuable tool to help you accept your imperfections and bolster your well-being. In the fast-paced, conflict-ridden world of school leadership, both learning and practicing self-compassion is paramount. Over time, the stresses of leadership can take a toll unless you learn to practice treating yourself with the same kindness and forgiveness you show to those you lead. It feels natural to feel compassion for others and oftentimes feels selfish to practice self-compassion. However, practicing self-compassion helps you honor yourself and your personal needs, and thus, it allows you to offer others more.

Coauthors Kristin Neff, a self-compassion researcher and speaker, and Christopher Germer (2018), a clinical psychologist and part-time lecturer, define *self-compassion* as "a practice in which we learn to be a good friend to ourselves when we need it most—to become an inner ally rather than an inner enemy" (p. 9). Neff and Germer (2018) describe self-compassion as being composed of three elements: (1) loving (self-kindness), (2) connected (common humanity), and (3) presence (mindfulness). A study by Filip Raes (2011), a professor of clinical psychology at the University of Leuven in Belgium, revealed that people with higher levels of self-compassion have a lower tendency of rumination (or obsessing over their thoughts). Raes (2011) links this to why these people report fewer symptoms of depression and anxiety. Neff and Germer (2018) write, "We can learn to embrace ourselves and our lives, despite inner and outer imperfections, and provide ourselves with the strength needed to thrive" (p. 1).

Although some feel self-compassion is self-indulgence, Neff (2015) negates this with her five research-based myths of self-compassion.

- **Self-compassion is self-pity:** Self-compassion is an antidote to self-pity. It allows people to accept difficult feelings with kindness and then let them go.

- **Self-compassion means weakness:** Studies suggest that how people relate to themselves through difficult times determines how well they can cope (Sbarra, Smith, & Mehl, 2012).

- **Self-compassion will make people complacent:** Researchers found that self-compassion strengthens accountability (Breines & Chen, 2012).

- **Self-compassion is narcissistic:** Neff (2015) differentiates between *self-esteem* and *self-compassion* when she writes, "Self-esteem requires feeling better than others, whereas self-compassion requires acknowledging that we share the human condition of imperfection."

- **Self-compassion is selfish:** When people are absorbed with self-judgment, they often have little to give others. Being good to themselves actually gives them more to offer others.

The following tips will guide you as you work toward mindfully developing your self-compassion.

- Take a moment to observe what you are feeling in this moment. Taking this moment to pause gives you the opportunity to respond rather than react to conflicts in the world of school leadership.

- Replace negative self-dialogue with affirmations or phrases you would use toward a loved one or colleague. For example, tell yourself, "I am enough" or "I will learn from this situation or mistake and move on."

- Process your feelings of self-doubt with a trusted friend or through journaling.

- Let go of the need to be perfect. Know that you are doing the best you can to serve your staff, students, and parents.

The following activity will help you learn to develop deeper self-compassion.

1. Think about a time when you were struggling, behaving unskillfully, or having self-deprecating thoughts. Perhaps you are a perfectionist, being much harder on yourself then you are on others. Reflect on the types of things you were saying to yourself. Notice if you exaggerated these thoughts in a negative manner.

2. Imagine someone you care about is struggling, behaving unskillfully, or having self-deprecating thoughts. Perhaps this is an educator with whom you work. Reflect on the types of things you would say to help the person manage difficult emotions. Notice the gentleness you would use to respond when others are hurting.

3. Place your hand on your heart and take a few deep, cleansing breaths.

4. Direct the gentle, kind thoughts you would offer a friend toward yourself.

5. Reflect on how it feels to show gentleness and compassion toward yourself.

At first, self-compassion may require some patience. With time and practice, self-compassion will become more natural. With self-compassion, you can learn to treat yourself as you would a loved one. By giving yourself the honor of self-compassion, you are developing the skills to extend that compassion to those you serve. Begin within by practicing self-compassion and self-awareness, and then spread the seeds of kindness toward others. The following fictional scenario demonstrates an example of this.

Karen, a high school dean of students, was born a people pleaser. Her parents often fought when she was a child, and she did her best to mediate each situation. Karen always did her best to do everything right so as not to "throw gasoline on the fires" at home. This tendency toward perfectionism carried into Karen's adult life and her role as dean of students. Anytime there was conflict, which was literally every workday, she replayed each interaction and found faults in herself. She never belittled others; she saved all that for herself.

When Karen learned about self-compassion, she teared up. This was a message for her. She sat quietly on her couch one evening and placed her hand on her heart. She breathed deeply in and out and considered the mean thoughts she always turned toward herself. Karen thought of her niece and the way she spoke to her. Karen then took those kind words and thoughts and turned them inward. She continued to breathe as tears rolled down her face. Finally, Karen wrote a few affirmations on sticky notes and hung them on her bathroom mirror: "I am worthy," "I am perfectly imperfect," and "I am becoming the best version of me!"

Mindful Movement

Active school leaders may wish for a more physical form of being mindful. After sitting in meetings and conducting classroom observations, it can feel wonderful to add movement into your day. The good news is that mindfulness isn't defined as sitting on a meditation cushion, although that is one type of mindfulness practice. *Mindful movement* is simply being present as you move your body; it is intentionally noticing the way your body feels as you move. By paying attention to your body, you can experience a sense of stillness and presence. This means leaving your headphones on the table and turning your awareness inward toward your body, breath, and mind. A 2018 study by Penn State researchers Chih-Hsiang Yang and David E. Conroy found mindful movement is associated with lowered stress, anxiety, and depression. Students reported feeling less stress when they were moving and had greater benefits when they were mindful at the time (Yang & Conroy, 2018). I describe various types of mindful movement in the following sections.

MINDFUL RUNNING

Mindful running means being present in the here and now while running. It includes paying attention to your senses, physical movement, running form, thoughts, and emotions. Instead of allowing yourself to zone out with music playing, mindful running brings awareness to your body and mind. This awareness during movement reduces stress, anxiety, and depression (Yang & Conroy, 2018).

Ashley Mateo (2020), a running coach and writer and editor for *Running World*, offers the following tips for mindful running.

- Before beginning your run, take a few minutes to calm yourself with mindful breathing (see page 36).

- Leave behind your headphones, GPS, and other tracking devices.

- As you run, pay attention to your breathing. If possible, breathe in and out through your nose, which creates a more relaxed state. Slow down if you are breathing too fast.

- Pay attention to where you are looking. Notice the path or road you are on. Notice the trees and the sky. Notice cars going by. By noticing your surroundings, you are being intentionally mindful.

- As you complete your run, take time for cool-down breathing. Focus on your breath for five to ten minutes.

MINDFUL WALKING

Closely related to mindful running is *mindful walking*. Mindful walking, like mindful running, has tremendous health benefits. It can improve self-awareness and reduce stress (Yang & Conroy, 2018). Research has shown walking combined with meditation reduces anxiety in youth (Edwards, Rosenbaum, & Loprinzi, 2018). Walking itself helped reduce anxiety in youth, and walkers achieved additional benefits if they meditated ten minutes before or after exercising (Edwards et al., 2018).

I adapted a few tips for mindful walking from Mark Bertin (2017), a developmental pediatrician and an author.

- Move at a calm, leisurely pace.

- Notice the sounds, textures, and sights using all your senses.

- As you breathe in and out, notice the fresh air filling your lungs.

- With each mindful step, notice the ground beneath your feet supporting you.

- If thoughts arise, gently bring your awareness back to the present moment.

MINDFUL EXERCISE

Whether you are lifting weights, stretching, or doing CrossFit, you can bring mindfulness to the activity. In a mindful workout, you bring your attention to the task at hand as opposed to zoning out. This includes focusing on your breath and physical sensations. A 2015 study of 398 Dutch participants found those who practiced mindfulness while exercising reporting feeling more satisfied (Tsafou, De Ridder, van Ee, & Lacroix, 2016).

The following are a few tips for mindful exercise.

- Warm up by focusing on your breathing. When you feel a shift to a sense of calmness, then it's time to begin your exercises.

- Pay attention to your breathing as you're working out. Inhale through your nostrils, feeling the air fill your lungs.

- Notice your physical sensations. Feel the strength of your muscles supporting your workout.

- Keep your purpose in mind. Perhaps you're exercising to reduce anxiety. Honor yourself for your self-care.

- Conclude your exercise with mindful breathing.

The following fictional scenario depicts how one administrator added mindful movements.

Chris, an assistant principal in charge of all disciplinary issues at a junior high school, had an especially trying day. She decided to go for a mindful run. Usually when she runs, Chris listens to a book on tape to distract her from the miles she's putting in. This time she intentionally left her earbuds in the car. Before heading down the running trail, Chris took a few cleansing breaths. As she started running, she paid attention to the sluggishness of her legs and her ragged breathing. Chris listened to the crunching sounds of her feet on the leafy gravel. As she got more into the flow of running, she noticed the colors of the leaves and the grayness of the sky. She silently thanked her legs and feet for their efforts. As Chris ended her run, she didn't immediately head home. Instead, she turned her focus to her breathing. She took a few minutes to pay attention to her in- and out-breaths. Chris made a mental note of her much-improved mood, deciding she would incorporate mindful movement more often into her busy schedule.

Mindful Writing

You can practice mindfulness in nearly everything you do, including mindful walking, mindful eating, mindful meditation, and mindful writing. A *mindful writing* practice, also referred to as *meditative journaling*, encourages peacefulness and develops self-awareness, which are paramount to mindfulness. According to the University of Virginia School of Medicine Mindfulness Center (n.d.), mindful writing "uses mindfulness to access the inner voice that we all have, which leads to the authentic self." A research study of forty-seven Arkansas State University students found that all participants perceived mindful writing as beneficial (Khramtsova &

Glascock, 2010). The students reported greater relaxation, positive thoughts, and peace of mind. One student shared that she "wished she had been exposed to these techniques years ago because they helped her to perform better academically and to feel better" (Khramtsova & Glascock, 2010, p. 217).

Mindful writing gives you a safe space to explore your feelings. Little is required to begin a mindfulness writing practice; you'll simply need a quiet space, a journal or notebook, and a pen. As an activity, journal writing shares some characteristics of mindfulness (Khramtsova & Glascock, 2010).

- It helps you focus on your inner world.

- It can increase positive thoughts.

- It can decrease negative thoughts.

- It has little or no cost.

- It can be done anywhere.

- It does not require special equipment.

You can use various prompts to guide your mindful writing. These prompts help you dive contemplatively into exploring your thoughts and feelings with openness and curiosity. As you write, turn your focus toward what you are feeling. Try not to censor your thoughts; instead, try writing the first things that come to mind. This will deepen your self-awareness. Ten mindfulness writing prompts are as follows.

1. What story is my inner dialogue revealing to me? Is there an alternate story I could be telling myself? What needs to shift in order to tell an alternate story?

2. What inner gifts do I bring to the world? How do these gifts serve my students, staff, family, and friends?

3. When am I most at peace? Where can I find more peace in my life?

4. How can I show up as my most authentic self?

5. How can I offer myself more compassion?

6. What are my intentions for this day?

7. What was the best part of my day?

8. In what areas do I need to forgive myself?

9. What am I passionate about as a school leader?

10. What are my best leadership qualities?

Like other mindfulness practices, mindful writing is more beneficial with commitment and practice. I recommend incorporating this practice one or more times weekly. It can help set the tone for the upcoming week. Mindful writing will help you notice things in different ways and make adjustments to live according to your values, such as the importance of showing compassion to others and yourself.

The following fictional scenario depicts one leader's use of mindful writing to help focus his personal values and bring peace to his life.

Connor, an elementary school principal, received a leather-bound journal years ago that he never used. He cracked it open and jotted down the following prompts: "Where is my life filled with inner light? How can I add more light to my life? Where can I better shine my inner light?" Connor set aside twenty uninterrupted minutes to write. He allowed a free flow of ideas as he wrote. He didn't edit his thoughts or feelings, but allowed them to just show up in his writing. When Connor finished, he looked over his writing and was surprised by some of the insights he gleaned in such a short time.

Summary

Mindfulness practice is, at least at first, an inside job. This chapter detailed ten mindfulness practices for both experienced and inexperienced practitioners to strengthen mindfulness *within*. Whether practicing mindful breathing, mindful meditation, or mindful movement, school leaders have many tools at their disposal to build or strengthen their mindfulness practice. This chapter provided examples of how leaders might incorporate these tools into their daily personal and professional lives.

In chapter 3, you'll learn how to extend your mindfulness practice to those you serve as a school or district leader.

Reflection Questions

Take a moment to respond to the following reflection questions, either in thought or in writing, before moving on to the next chapter.

1. Where can I find moments to incorporate mindful breathing into my schedule?

2. What are the benefits of mindful meditation? How can I include meditation in my day-to-day life?

3. Where can I find time to unplug from technology at work? At home?

4. On a scale of 1 to 10, what is my level of self-compassion? What have I learned about self-compassion to help me personally and professionally?

CHAPTER 3

Reaching Out

Leadership . . . is not an affair of the head.
Leadership is an affair of the heart.

—James M. Kouzes and Barry Z. Posner

A school leader's role has grown much more complex than it was historically. Leaders are now tasked with collaboratively creating and promoting a shared vision to improve the learning and well-being of all students, and they are responsible for building a culture where stakeholders show respect and openness toward one another while working toward the vision. Responsibilities of the leader, to name a few, include building trust, collaboration, and partnerships with families and communities, and developing shared leadership. All of these responsibilities require tremendous talent and heart from the leader. This is where mindfulness toward others comes in.

In addition to transforming people personally, mindfulness has the power to transform their leadership. When leaders mindfully build connections with those they work with, and when they are present and aware of those they serve, they can lead from a place of excellence. Mindfulness has been shown to increase leadership effectiveness by helping leaders focus on the present moment, act with intentionality, and have greater self-compassion (Reb, Sim, Chintakananda, & Bhave, 2015). *Mindful presence* is a deep practice you can cultivate over time. Those mindful leaders serve can sense a powerful difference in the leaders' presence. Mindful leaders are less reactive, instead choosing to act based on their values and principles (Stedham & Skaar, 2019).

While the mindfulness practices shared in the previous chapter (page 35) focused on beginning within, this chapter offers seven specific tools to help school leaders reach out and extend mindful awareness and presence in interpersonal relationships and experiences. It presents research relating to each tool before describing how to perform each practice. The chapter concludes with reflection questions relating to these mindfulness tools.

Seven Mindfulness Tools for Reaching Out

There is empirical evidence that the mindfulness of leaders aids in the well-being of stakeholders (Arendt, Verdorfer, & Kugler, 2019; Reb, 2014). The seven tools that follow help leaders lead from a place of mindfulness, offering compassion, calmness, grace, and kindness. Although all these practices are valuable in leadership, I recommend you begin with *compassionate leadership*, as this underscores every aspect of reaching out mindfully.

Compassionate Leadership

Leading with compassion begins when people understand their common humanity. Everyone wants to love and be loved. Everyone wants to experience peace and joy. Everyone experiences frustrations and hardships. Everyone suffers at various times in their lives. This is where compassion comes in.

Compassion is defined as having an awareness of the needs of others and a desire to help (Jiménez, 2021). Research from the Potential Project revealed that employees who perceive their leader as compassionate have 36 percent higher organizational commitment and 34 percent higher job satisfaction, and are 54 percent happier with their leader (Carter, 2022). Yet, a Gallup survey reveals only 45 percent of employees feel their employer cares about their well-being (Harter, 2020). Mindfulness practices focused on compassionate leadership can help leaders ensure their staffs know they care about their well-being, even as those leaders demand excellence from their staffs' teaching and students' learning.

A mindfulness practice known as *metta meditation* comes from Buddhist tradition from over 2,600 years ago and is a proven way to strengthen your compassion for yourself and others (Chowdhury, 2019). *Metta*, translated from Pali, means *loving-kindness* (Chowdhury, 2019). Researcher Helen Weng and colleagues (2013) conducted a University of Wisconsin-Madison study, which revealed that training adults in a loving-kindness meditation makes them more compassionate and altruistic. Participants were provided a thirty-minute compassion meditation they listened to once a day for two weeks. A functional MRI revealed those who participated in the compassion meditation training showed increased activity in the neural networks involved in understanding the suffering of others and emotional regulation. "It's kind of like weight training," Weng says. "We found that people can actually build up their compassion 'muscle' and respond to others' suffering with care and a desire to help" (as cited Ladwig, 2013).

The following steps outline the metta meditation practice.

1. Begin by sitting in a chair with your feet planted on the floor and hands on your thighs. Alternatively, you may choose to lie down.

2. Allow your eyes to close. Take a few deep belly breaths. Relax your body.

3. Begin by sending loving kindness toward yourself. Imagine filling your body, mind, and spirit with loving energy. Breathe in loving energy and breathe out tension. Repeat these positive messages silently to yourself.

    » "May I be safe."

    » "May I be happy."

    » "May I be healthy."

    » "May I be peaceful."

    Allow feelings of warmth and self-appreciation to envelop you. Bask in these feelings for a few minutes.

4. Send feelings of loving kindness toward someone you love. Extend loving energy toward that person for a few breaths. Send good wishes to this person by repeating the following positive messages silently.

    » "May you be safe."

    » "May you be happy."

    » "May you be healthy."

    » "May you be peaceful."

▶

5. Bring to mind a person toward whom you feel neutral. This could be an employee, a neighbor, or an acquaintance. Send good wishes toward this neutral person by silently repeating the following mantras.

   » "May you be safe."

   » "May you be happy."

   » "May you be healthy."

   » "May you be peaceful."

6. Direct your loving-kindness meditation toward someone with whom you have difficulties. Like you, this person wants to experience well-being. Send good wishes toward this person by silently repeating the following.

   » "May you be safe."

   » "May you be happy."

   » "May you be healthy."

   » "May you be peaceful."

7. When you are ready, gently open your eyes. Notice how you feel after your metta meditation. You may experience more positive emotions, including happiness and greater compassion toward yourself and others. At first, it may prove difficult to send good wishes toward someone with whom you have difficulties. Try not to judge your feelings. With continued practice, you will likely notice a shift toward more compassion, even for those you consider difficult.

Feel free to include variations of the preceding statements. You may wish to close your metta meditation by extending well-being to all sentient beings. Over time and with practice, your compassion muscle will strengthen.

The following fictional scenario is an example of implementing metta meditation.

Julia, a high school dean of students, was irritated with the principal. She didn't want to look for a new job, so she knew she needed to develop some compassion toward her boss. Each evening before going to sleep, Julia sat for ten minutes and used the practice of metta meditation. At first, she felt as if she were faking the good wishes she was sending toward the principal. However, she stayed with the practice. In just two weeks, Julia noticed she had less self-criticism and more compassion toward others, including her boss.

Leadership Meditation

Serving as a school leader can often be overwhelming. It is easy for a leader to be swept up by the day-to-day minutiae of managing task after task. This can cause you to lose sight of the bigger purpose of your role as a leader.

Leadership meditation—meditating on what it means to be a leader and what type of leader you wish to embody—helps set the tone for successful, supportive, and compassionate leadership. Leadership meditations can strengthen your self-awareness, focus, purpose, and emotional intelligence (Insight Timer, n.d.). Bringing an awareness of those you serve and your overall mission to the forefront of your mind can help center you on leading purposefully and mindfully. Your ability to lead others is improved because, through meditating on leadership and meditating in general, you will recover faster, manage your own emotions more thoughtfully, and stay calm in difficult situations (Daskal, n.d.).

I adapted the following leadership meditation from leadership expert and mindfulness teacher Tovi Scruggs-Hussein (2021).

1. Sit in a comfortable position. Gently close your eyes. Breathing in and out, allow your jaw and shoulders to soften. Allow your breathing to come to a natural rhythm.
2. Focus on setting the tone for your leadership. Consider saying the following to yourself: "I see myself being the very best in my unique leadership. I am a walking, breathing manifestation of the vision, mission, and purpose for those I serve. I hold this responsibility with reverence and integrity."
3. Breathe that mantra in and out for a few moments.
4. Take a moment to honor yourself as a leader. Understand that you can create the presence and tone you want for your leadership.
5. Invite in the qualities you'd like to experience as a leader: wisdom, compassion, kindness, confidence, and so on.
6. Conclude your leadership meditation with a sense of gratitude for yourself as a leader and for serving a greater purpose.
7. Allow your eyes to gently open.

It is indeed worth taking the time to meditate on the bigger picture of your leadership. Focusing on the leadership qualities you want to embody helps anchor them into your daily practice. It helps instill your greater purpose.

The following fictional scenario shows a leader implementing this practice.

Jacob, a middle school principal, was stuck in the doldrums of a cold January. At work, he felt little of the optimism he had started the school year with and was dreading the long haul until summer break. For the remainder of the year, he decided to start each school week with a fifteen-minute leadership meditation. Jacob found the practice renewed his sense of purpose and intention. It helped set the tone for showing up with passion for serving others with his talents and skills.

Mindful Listening

One of the most beneficial gifts school leaders can give is the gift of listening with presence and awareness. When leaders are willing to listen, they allow greater connections and understanding (Fletcher, 2022). Mindful listening allows those they serve to feel truly heard. This openness can help to create a safe space for staff to share their thoughts with leaders.

Mindful listening is defined as "listening for understanding as opposed to waiting your turn to speak" (Brown & Olson, 2015, p. 116). Rather than letting extraneous thoughts distract them, mindful leaders show up with a receptive heart. Without mindful listening, leaders' attention is often scattered, which gives the impression they do not really care what the speaker has to say. Mindful teacher and author Oren Jay Sofer (2018) describes mindful listening in this manner:

> To truly listen depends on a kind of inner silence. It requires that we empty ourselves and make space to receive something new. This entails a fundamental letting go of self-centeredness. We have to be willing to put down our own thoughts, views, and feelings temporarily to truly listen. It's a wholehearted, embodied receptivity that lies at the core of both communication and contemplative practice.

Research shows people spend approximately 45 percent of their time listening, yet the average person retains only 25 to 50 percent of the conversation after just a few minutes (Drinko, 2021; Shafir, 2000). This is partially because people often spend time planning their responses, being distracted, or even interrupting, according to author and researcher Ximena Vengoechea (2021). Therefore, learning to listen mindfully is extremely valuable for school leaders.

According to Steve J. Scott (2017), author, owner, and chief creator of the website Develop Good Habits (https://developgoodhabits.com), the benefits of mindful listening include the following.

- **Deeper relationships.** The more you authentically listen to people, the more you will understand their viewpoints. You will gradually get to know them on a more personal level, which will strengthen and deepen your relationship. For school leaders, this can occur with all stakeholders.

- **Improved self-awareness.** Through mindful listening, you will be more in tune with your own reactions and thoughts as well as your physical presence. You may become aware of your own biases while listening to truly hear and understand. In the school setting, this may provide a broader range of possible solutions and greater creativity.

- **Enhanced empathy.** You will increase your ability to understand other people's situation by truly listening to what they are saying. Mindful listening involves giving your energy and time to truly hear and feel with others.

- **Improved focus.** Mindful listening quiets the mind over time, providing a stronger ability to attend to the conversations in which you are engaged. With the multitude of tasks and people demanding school leaders' attention, it can be easy to become distracted. With practice, mindful listening helps you attend more deeply to what others are saying.

- **Increased productivity.** Mindful listening allows you to build on what other people are saying. Therefore, you waste little time by getting off track.

- **Improved workplace morale.** When people feel heard, they feel as if their ideas matter. This helps them remain loyal to their cause.

Mindful listening can have a profound effect on your staff. Researchers Guy Itzchakov and Avi N. Kluger (2018) conducted a study, which found employees paired with good listeners felt less anxiety, greater self-awareness, and deeper understanding about attitudes on varied topics. Further, mindful listening allows employees to be more open to others' ideas for projects and solutions. This may allow leaders to better choose the right people to serve on various committees or lead projects.

Mindful listening doesn't come easy at first. However, much like the beginning-within skills from chapter 2 (page 35), mindful listening is a skill you can develop with practice. You must begin with the intention of being fully present while listening, then interrupt your own inner dialogue to truly hear what the other person is saying. Try to be aware of your immediate biases or reactions. You may notice you are planning a response instead of listening. As you become aware of your inner dialogue, gently come back to listening. You can train yourself to bring your attention fully to the person speaking, rather than focusing on what has already occurred or what may occur. This allows you to focus on and understand the speaker to the best of your ability.

Even when tensions are high, you can shift the energy by your presence and non-judgment through mindful listening. Imagine an extremely angry student who just had a heated conflict in the hallway. As you meet with her, you turn your focus and attention to what she has to say. You tune out the other tasks waiting for you. Instead of jumping to a reprimand, as you have in the past, you are open to hearing the student's thoughts. Because she feels listened to, she is more likely to show self-reflect and accept the consequences for her actions. Just bringing this type of presence to a situation can encourage a sense of calmness and understanding. This is the power of mindful listening. It is similar to meditation practice, in which you focus on the present moment rather than the past or future.

The following steps will help improve your ability to listen mindfully.

1. Set aside an appropriate amount of time to give your full attention to the speaker. Reschedule the conversation, if necessary, to ensure you provide adequate time.

2. Prior to the meeting, center yourself by taking a few calming, grounding breaths. This time to pause can help you bring a calmer focus and clearer attention.

3. When the meeting starts, give your full presence to the speaker.

   » Look at the speaker on the same level, sitting eye-to-eye rather than towering over the person.

   » Leave your smartphone out of sight.

   » Adjust your posture to show openness and attentiveness. Similar to a meditation posture, you should sit upright yet in a relaxed way. You want to avoid crossing your arms, as this can signify being closed to what the person is saying.

> » Listen without preparing your own response. As best-selling author, educator, and speaker Stephen R. Covey (2020) states, "The biggest communication problem is we do not listen to understand. We listen to reply" (p. 274).
>
> » Show you are truly listening with verbal and nonverbal cues, such as saying, "I hear what you are saying," and nodding when appropriate.
>
> **4.** Ask open-ended questions as needed. These may include, "Can you tell me more?"
>
> **5.** Paraphrase to understand. This may include, "What I hear you saying is . . . ."
>
> **6.** Be mindful of your own thoughts, feelings, and emotions. Once you notice them, bring yourself back to the information the person is sharing with you. This is similar to bringing yourself back to your breath during meditation.
>
> **7.** Respond respectfully. Take a moment to pause before responding. It's OK to ask for more time before making decisions.

By quieting your inner dialogue and showing up with deep presence, you allow the speaker to feel fully understood. Deep listening makes a tremendous difference in the lives of school leaders.

The following fictional scenario depicts a school leader listening mindfully.

John, a middle school principal, was meeting with a parent of a troubled student. The parent, Mrs. Hall, was one of the parents with whom he regularly had difficulties. John had cleared his schedule to give her thirty minutes of his time. Prior to the meeting, he set his cell phone in his desk drawer and took a few cleansing breaths. John greeted Mrs. Hall warmly and sat diagonally from her. As she began her litany of everything wrong with the school, John could feel himself tense up. He felt defensive. Noting this about himself, he took a deep breath and nodded attentively. He intentionally focused on perceiving how she must feel as a frustrated parent.

When Mrs. Hall finished, John paused before responding. He wanted to now focus on solutions. "What is going well for your son in our school?" he asked. After a few more negative comments, Mrs. Hall admitted that her son, Caleb, loved his art teacher, and that it was the one thing keeping him in school.

"I agree with both you and Caleb. Mrs. Bourgeois is not only a great art teacher but also a great human!" John's brain went into solution mode. "No promises," he said, "but what if I looked into a way to possibly have Caleb take art every day? Of course, I'd need to check with Mrs. Bourgeois and get back to you." Tears sprang into Mrs. Hall's eyes. She admitted it would certainly make getting Caleb to come to school easier. At the end of the meeting, Mrs. Hall thanked John for hearing her viewpoint and looking for ways to help her son. Upon reflecting, John knew mindful listening helped him stay present and open.

Mindful Speaking

Words are powerful. The power of a school leader's words can build a common vision and shared purpose. You can conduct all your conversations—even the difficult ones—from a space of mindfulness. The words you choose and your manner of expressing them matter. These words set the tone for employees, students, family members, and the larger community.

There is a Buddhist saying: "When meditating, watch your mind. When in the world, watch your words" (as cited in Fronsdal, 2022). *Mindful speaking* is speaking with awareness of the words you are choosing, the intention you are holding, and your overall tone and body language. It involves pausing to consider the effect your words will have on others. Are your words necessary, kind, and purposeful? Are you speaking from your heart?

Your intent as a school leader should always tie into the larger goal of serving the needs of your students through a shared vision and purpose. Even in the simplest of conversations, you can stay centered on the idea that *you're here for the students*. Your tone and body language should reflect both optimism and calmness, especially in difficult situations. It is important to realize that school leaders must model what they expect of others. While speaking mindfully, notice the receptivity, or lack thereof, of those with whom you are interacting. It may be necessary to adjust your wording and offer ample time for questions.

In the context of school leadership, everything you say should indeed be necessary, kind, and purposeful. For example, you may have the difficult task of dismissing an employee, but you can do this with a kind, calm demeanor and thoughtful, purposeful word choices. In essence, mindful speaking includes grounding yourself with a thoughtful intention. What would you like to accomplish with this interaction? How will your words be beneficial? Further, mindful speaking involves bringing an awareness to staying open with your body, spirit, and mind.

Prior to speaking, if time and space allow, take yourself through the following four steps.

1. Breathe deeply in and out a few times, expanding and contracting your belly as you breathe. This is easy to accomplish in your office, restroom, or even while seated among others. It's a subtle expansion and contraction others generally don't notice.

2. Ground yourself with your intention. Be aware of the purpose of your words.

3. Bring an awareness of how you care for your audience. Feel goodwill toward your audience. Even if you're dissatisfied with recent school scores on the state examination, it is still possible to expand your heart with feelings of appreciation and goodwill.

4. Pause briefly to think about what you want to say.

Once centered, it is time to share your thoughts aloud using the following five steps.

1. Speak from your heart. Be genuine in your choice of words and thoughts.

2. Use eye contact and maintain open body language.

3. Use purposeful pauses. Pauses allow time for the listeners to receive and process the information you provide. Pauses also can add emphasis to key points you make. Further, pausing allows you time to gauge the audience's receptiveness and understanding.

4. As you speak, be aware of your audience's receptiveness. Notice if they're engaged or looking away. Notice if they are nodding in agreement or having sidebar conversations. Taking time to notice your audience allows you to make adjustments to what you're sharing.

5. Leave time to answer questions and clarify your meaning.

The following fictional scenario provides an example of speaking mindfully.

Kelly is a principal of an elementary school. He is welcoming his staff back from a much-deserved spring break and wants to set the intention for the remaining days of school. Prior to spring break, Kelly noticed the majority of his staff just going through the motions of work and lacking enthusiasm for teaching. In fairness, it had been the most difficult year in his tenure as a leader.

Before planning the agenda for his upcoming staff meeting, Kelly took a few minutes to breathe deeply and consider what his teachers needed to finish the year with strength and enthusiasm. He knew his first few sentences in the meeting could help set the tone for the rest of the year. He took a minute to visualize numerous teachers and consider what they might need. He reflected on their individual and collective strengths. He breathed out gratitude for the gift they are to the students. Kelly then set his intention: *To motivate our educators to finish strong, and to be there with soulfulness and purpose for the children with whom we are entrusted.*

Only then did Kelly take out a pen and begin to jot down notes. He looked at his wall at a quote he had printed from the internet and started writing.

> Teachers who are tired, worn out, and utterly exhausted are mostly likely making a bigger difference than they will ever know.

From there, the words came straight from his heart.

> I know what you're doing often seems thankless and repetitive. Trust me when I tell you every educator has this feeling from time to time. As we finish the last forty-five days of this school year, I invite you to finish strong, to show up each day with soulfulness and purpose for each student whose parents have entrusted to our care.

> Please take a moment to pause each day for the rest of this year to realize you are central to each student's life. What you do matters. I invite you to celebrate the small wins: your students mastered paragraph writing, a struggling student learned to write his name, or you led an amazing discussion about bullying. Teachers, you matter! You matter to each student, each day. And I am humbled to serve as your leader. Let's encourage each other to finish strong, to never forget what we do matters!

On the morning of the staff meeting, Kelly took a mindful moment to glance around the room at the educators present. He allowed himself to feel love and appreciation for each of them before beginning the meeting. He made eye contact with numerous educators. Speaking from his heart, he shared the sentiments he had written and committed to memory the day before.

Kelly purposefully included pauses, allowing time for his words to sink in. He noticed which teachers were soaking up his words and which ones seemed indifferent. He mentally noted to check in with those who seemed less receptive. After he finished speaking, Kelly opened the meeting to questions from the educators. When there were no questions, he paused a moment before he moved into the agenda. As the meeting ended, Kelly teared up. He took a deep breath and again made eye contact with several teachers before saying, "I'll close with another quote from the internet hanging on my office wall: *A teacher takes a hand, opens a mind, and touches the heart.* And for this, I thank you. I am here to help you finish strong."

With practice, it becomes easier to set a clear intention and speak from your heart. The benefits of speaking mindfully are that you will likely be thoughtful with your words and have improved relationships, decreased tension, and fewer regrets.

Mindfulness in Difficult Conversations

Difficult conversations are a part of a school leader's role. The district-level school board or local education authority expects school leaders to have the skills to provide performance feedback, non-renew staff members, and give students disciplinary consequences. These conversations often bring up challenging emotions and strong feelings, which can make leaders, as well as the people they're speaking with, uncomfortable. So how can leaders mindfully have difficult conversations?

Mindfulness in difficult conversations is about making the conscious decision to continue being mindful even when everything about the situation you're in feels in conflict with mindfulness practices. Your mind is racing, your heart is beating faster, and you're unsure of the best course of action. Or maybe you feel angry and want to lash out. Fight-or-flight responses are part of people's genetic makeup, and while everyone in the building—from adults to students—must self-manage them (or learn to do so), it's especially incumbent on leaders to maintain a sense of mindfulness when conversations are at their most challenging. Mindfulness reminds leaders it is possible to discuss difficult topics while exercising openness, compassion, and respect. As Buddhist monk and author Thich Nhat Hanh (2013) states, "The energy of mindfulness is a necessary ingredient in healthy communication" (pp. 4–5).

The following steps can guide you in having difficult conversations mindfully.

1. Prepare your environment. You'll often know a difficult conversation is coming before it begins. Ensure there will be no interruptions. Set the chairs angled toward each other as opposed to face-to-face, as

this is less confrontational. If there are more than two people having the conversation, aim to seat those in disagreement at an angle. Put your smartphone away.

2. Become aware of your intention. Reflect on the purpose of the discussion by asking yourself, "What is important in this conversation?" Think of the most appropriate way to approach the conversation. Think about using peaceful language to convey your thoughts.

3. Before the difficult conversation begins, take a few minutes to center and calm yourself. If you've been caught off guard and are unable to prepare, you can still take a moment to breathe in and out through your nose while keeping your belly soft.

4. Begin the conversation by clearly and compassionately stating the purpose of the conversation and the facts.

5. Continue to be aware of your breathing and body sensations throughout the conversation.

6. Give the other person the space to react to what you've said by listening mindfully (see page 68). Demonstrate compassion and empathy as you listen. This includes maintaining eye contact, nodding, and paraphrasing. Provide space for the person to express his, her, or their feelings. Often, the act of listening can give the speaker a sense of calmness, even in highly charged situations. If you cannot come to an agreement together, then you as the school leader (or superintendent) need to ensure the decision aligns with the school's vision and current research in the area. In certain situations, someone may be openly contentious or hostile. In this case, it is best to end the meeting and reschedule at a later time, with a request for all present to remain civil. If this is impossible, you may require mediation.

7. Conclude the conversation by acknowledging the outcome and thanking the person for his, her, or their time. If the resolution was unacceptable to both parties, it is important to still thank the person, while providing the option of reconvening at a later date if more time is needed.

8. After the difficult conversation, take a moment to reflect on what went well and what you could improve. You might consider what you need to do differently in similar situations.

The following fictional scenario provides an example of mindfully having a difficult conversation.

Emma, the principal of a middle school, has a difficult conversation slated for first thing in the morning. She is about to meet with an educator, Brianna, who routinely comes late to staff meetings or fails to show up at all. Prior to the meeting, Emma took time to form a clear understanding of the purpose of the meeting, the supporting evidence, and her intention. The purpose of the meeting is clear in her mind: *To explain to Brianna the expectations of educators attending staff meetings and being on time to meetings, as well as to document the meeting in Brianna's records.* The supporting evidence includes the dates of missed meetings as well as the dates and times Brianna arrived late.

As Emma sits in her office prior to the upcoming meeting, she turns off her cell phone and then tucks it out of sight. Next, she takes a moment to ground herself with deep belly breathing. She brings to mind her intention: *To be clear about explaining the expectation that Brianna attend staff meetings and be on time to meetings, as well as taking the time to truly listen and understand Brianna's viewpoint.* Emma takes a moment to consider the many areas in which Brianna thrives as an educator, bringing herself to a place of goodwill toward her. Emma notes that Brianna is a very motivating and engaging educator who sets high expectations for her students, which helps them thrive under her care. When she invites Brianna into her office, Emma feels both a sense of peace and preparedness.

"Thank you for meeting with me," Emma says with a genuine smile. "Please have a seat." As Brianna sits down, Emma purposefully chooses to sit diagonally from her to be less confrontational. She relaxes her body and turns toward Brianna, making eye contact. "How are you doing today?"

"I'm fine. Let's just get this over with," says Brianna. "I have important things to do."

Emma, sensing a rising irritation in herself, takes a calming breath before continuing the meeting. She leans forward slightly and makes eye contact. She speaks from her heart as she says, "Before we dive into this meeting, I want to take a moment to thank you for what you do for your students. Your engaging style keeps them motivated, even with the most challenging content. I also appreciate the way you set high expectations for your students."

"Glad I'm doing something right," jokes Brianna.

Emma observes the passive-aggressiveness in Brianna's words and tone but lets them slide away, instead remaining focused on her purpose. "Now, I'd like to get to the purpose of today's meeting, which is twofold: first, for me to remind you of the importance of attendance at our staff meetings as well as the importance of showing up on time for them. Second, to understand your point of view. Our monthly staff meetings are a requirement of being an educator here. I have noted that you've missed two meetings on September 7 and October 5. And then at yesterday's meeting, you arrived fifteen minutes late." Emma notices Brianna's eyes rolling. She allows herself another pause for a belly breath before continuing. "Can you help me understand your situation?" At this point, Emma centers herself while thinking it is time to listen mindfully.

"I have two aging parents. My role as their adult child is to make sure they are getting their medications, eating, bathing regularly, and getting to and from all doctors' appointments. My dad needs cataract surgery, and my mom has dementia. They are much more of a priority to me than our stupid staff meetings," Brianna states emphatically.

The word *stupid* could easily be a trigger for Emma, but she quickly recognizes the need for compassion for Brianna's difficult position. Everyone reacts differently to intense life circumstances like these, and this context makes Brianna's anger and frustration understandable, despite being inappropriate. Emma lets herself embrace compassion for the Brianna's circumstances, makes eye contact, and replies, "Oh, Brianna. I had no idea. I understand how difficult that must be. That must be very time consuming and stressful."

"That's the understatement of the century," Brianna states sarcastically.

Emma pauses. She takes a centering breath before continuing. "I'm sorry you're under so much duress. It is difficult to have so much responsibility," she says honestly. "Perhaps we can brainstorm strategies to meet both sets of expectations. Let's consider ways for you to provide the help your parents need as well as for you to be at staff meetings on time."

"It's simply not possible," Brianna says defensively.

"Have you considered a home health agency to help you out?"

"My parents would never go for that. They aren't going to allow complete strangers into their home."

"I understand what you're saying. Are there relatives or friends who could pitch in on the afternoons we have staff meetings?" Emma asks.

"Maybe. Maybe not," responds Brianna. Emma notices that Brianna anxiously glances at the clock.

"I know you need to get back to your classroom soon, Brianna. And I'm sorry you're feeling stressed. I'd like to help you continue to find ways to support your parents. As we end this meeting, I'd like to give you a little leeway considering your situation, although to do this, I need to ask two things of you. First, if you simply can't make it on time, can you send me a text to give me a heads-up? Also, I'd like to ask you to continue to seek friends or relatives who can help you out when you have staff meetings."

"I can do that."

"Do you have any questions for me?" Emma asks.

"Nope."

"Thank you, Brianna, for your time. I'll document our meeting and give you a copy. Again, remember to send me a text if you're going to be late. Also, try to find additional support to help out with your parents. Please know, I am always here for you if you need to talk or vent any frustrations."

"Thank you," mumbles Brianna as she leaves Emma's office.

Emma takes a moment to reflect on the conversation. She takes a few deep belly breaths. She considers what went well and what she could improve. She wishes she had scheduled the meeting at a time when Brianna wouldn't feel rushed. Emma is pleased that she clearly stated her intention. She makes a mental note to check in with Brianna on a regular basis to offer moral support. Emma then documents the meeting for her records before attending to her other duties as a school leader.

This vignette illustrates an example of when school leaders need to be more accommodating toward employees. In other situations, you may need to hold a firmer line. Each situation is unique, but through mindful communication, you can often reach a solution.

By using mindful leadership skills (including centering yourself, setting your intention, listening, and showing up with compassion), you will become more at ease when having difficult conversations. This does not mean you are a pushover. It does mean you will be more centered and calmer while conducting difficult conversations, as the scenario with Emma and Brianna demonstrates. As author Holly Weeks states, "Handling a difficult conversation well is not just a skill, it is an act of courage" (in Knight, 2015).

Common Ground Through Mindful Leadership

Every day as a school leader, you will face many types of conflict. Conflict is inevitable. You can call on your leadership skills to break through the conflicts and find common ground. *Finding common ground* is about building bridges between two or more people in conflict, allowing them to feel valued, empowered, and heard as they come to a resolution. This does not mean those involved must agree about everything; rather, it means finding topics or opinions in common (or at least reaching a consensus) that enables moving forward.

Seeking common ground helps you remain open to various opinions and possibilities. As Baptist minister and activist Martin Luther King Jr. stated, "A genuine leader is not a searcher for consensus but a molder of consensus" (Goodreads, n.d.). Through mindfulness, school leaders can better establish centeredness and connection, allowing for more creative solutions in complex school dilemmas. For example, staff members may have highly intense disagreements about class schedules. But by remaining calm and open throughout the discussion, staff members can achieve better solutions. According to leadership coach and best-selling author John C. Maxwell (2010), "Connecting is the ability to identify with people and relate to them in a way that increases your influence with them" (p. 3).

The following steps will help you lead others toward finding common ground through mindful leadership.

1. Before meeting, take a moment to find a sense of centeredness and calmness. Close your eyes for a few minutes. Take a few belly breaths. Allow your face and shoulders to soften.

2. As you begin the meeting, bring the focus to the outcome. You might consider posing the following questions: "How can we create something good from our cooperation? What is it we all want to accomplish? How can we remain student-centered in our discussion?"

3. Next, bring the attention to why it is important to reach that outcome.

4. As the conversation continues, be open to differing opinions. Be curious. Be mindful when you feel yourself shutting down from differing opinions. Bring yourself back to openness.

5. Listen mindfully (see page 68). Pause to hear other viewpoints. Often in disagreements, people just want to be heard.

6. Use open body language as you speak and listen. Use eye contact. Smile when appropriate.

7. Stay centered with a few mindful breaths throughout the meeting.

8. Be willing to pause and ask others to take a moment before proceeding.

9. While staying open, search for common connections and agreements. If the situation is especially difficult, it is important to bring the focus back to what is best for the students and what the research supports. Verbalize and act on commonalities.

10. Close the meeting with a summary of commonalities. Express gratitude toward all participants for their willingness to establish common ground.

The following fictional scenario demonstrates a mindful school leader helping to build common ground between an upset parent and a classroom educator.

Allison, an elementary school principal, will soon be meeting with a parent of a third-grade student and a classroom educator. The parent, Mrs. Martinez, refuses to allow her son to do homework. She believes his time spent in school is when he should complete all schoolwork. The teacher, Mr. Harvey, is a firm believer in using homework as an extension of the day's learning. Since the meeting might be tense at first, Allison takes a few minutes to mindfully center herself. She sits down and places her hands on her belly and breathes in and out several times, noticing the rise and fall of her abdomen. She allows her jaw to soften and her shoulders to relax. Allison then focuses on her role in helping the teacher and parent work together for the betterment of the student.

Soon after, she invites in Mrs. Martinez, who is Carlos's mother. "Welcome," Allison says warmly while gesturing for Mrs. Martinez to have a seat. "It's wonderful to see you again." As Mr. Harvey enters the room, Allison gestures for him to take the seat diagonal to Mrs. Martinez. "Welcome, Mr. Harvey," Allison says with a smile.

"Our outcome for this meeting is to reach an understanding that will best support Carlos and his learning regarding homework. I'd like to invite both of you to spend our time together in a spirit of cooperation and ask that each of you bring a willingness to listen to one another," Allison begins. "Mrs. Martinez, would you like to share your specific concerns?"

"Definitely! Carlos has soccer practice after school three days a week and piano practice another day. By the time he gets home, he's exhausted. He's only eight years old, and he needs time to relax and be with his family. It's ridiculous what this teacher is expecting of him!" she shares while pointing a finger at Mr. Harvey.

Allison glances at Mr. Harvey to assess how he took the finger-wagging. Sensing he's fine, Allison asks him to share his concerns. Emphatically, Mr. Harvey states, "Homework is a necessary part of the learning process, Mrs. Martinez. It does two things. First, it reinforces and helps cement the processes we worked on that day in the classroom. Second, it helps students develop the study habits they will need for success in the upper grades." When Mrs. Martinez rolls her eyes, Mr. Harvey sighs.

Noting the need to show some commonality, Allison states, "It is clear we all have something in common: we all want what is best for Carlos."

"Since I'm his mother, I will decide what is best for Carlos," Mrs. Martinez declares unequivocally.

Allison pauses to center herself with a calming breath. She smiles sincerely at Mrs. Martinez.

"We both understand your concerns," states Allison. "We do have high expectations for our students. Perhaps you could help us by explaining the amount of time Carlos is spending on his homework."

"Some nights, he doesn't finish until after 9:00 p.m.! He spends up to two hours a night on homework!" Mrs. Martinez says exasperatedly. "He often can't finish it because he doesn't understand the concepts you want set in concrete."

"Two hours? I rarely, if ever, give more than an hour of homework," Mr. Harvey explains defensively.

"Tell that to my son when he's still trying to finish it past his bedtime!"

Allison intervenes. "Let's take a moment just to pause." She breathes in and out, in and out. Allison makes eye contact with each of them before continuing. "It's important to keep in mind that we all have Carlos's best interests in mind. We all want him to be successful as a student and in life." She smiles warmly at both of them.

Allison continues, "Perhaps we can meet somewhere in the middle."

"How?" Mrs. Martinez asks in a brusque tone.

"I agree that homework is important to solidify the concepts learned at school. I also agree that children need time to rest and relax. A guideline from the parent-teacher association and National Education Association states that ten minutes per grade level is appropriate for students," Allison suggests.

"But I can't guarantee my homework will take the third-graders just thirty minutes," states Mr. Harvey.

"Exactly my point!" scoffs Mrs. Martinez.

"Let's look for common ground here," suggests Allison. She takes another purposeful pause. "Perhaps, we could use the PTA's suggestion as a place to start. What would you both think of the idea of agreeing to thirty minutes of homework, whether or not Carlos finishes it?" She makes eye contact with each of them. Allison notices Mr. Harvey's arms are crossed but remains hopeful that he'll give a little.

Mrs. Martinez seems reluctant at first and then nods. "No more than thirty minutes," she states while wagging her finger once again in Mr. Harvey's direction.

"Fair enough," he says, "but no less. If he finishes early, you need to make sure he spends time reading. That's the only way to build the foundation Carlos needs to be successful."

"Can we all agree that thirty minutes is fair? Can we give try it and see how it goes?" asks Allison, looking first at Mrs. Martinez and then at Mr. Harvey.

"How do I grade what isn't finished?" asks Mr. Harvey.

"We can discuss this further, but I'm thinking that you can grade what Carlos completes," suggests Allison.

"I'm willing to try thirty minutes and see how it goes," says Mrs. Martinez. "But don't you even think about lowering his grade for any unfinished work!"

"Fine," says Mr. Harvey, tossing his hands up in the air.

"I want to take a moment to summarize what we've agreed on," states Allison. Once again, she makes eye contact with each of them. She purposefully pauses before summarizing. "We've agreed that thirty minutes of homework each evening is a fair expectation for Carlos's learning. After thirty minutes, he may stop his homework, and Mr. Harvey will grade the completed portion of the work. Unfinished homework will not count against him, although he will still be graded using in-class assessments for proficiency. Also, if he finishes early, he is expected to read until the thirty minutes is up. This seems like an appropriate amount of time since Carlos is achieving at his grade level in reading. Agreed?" She looks at Mrs. Martinez and then Mr. Harvey.

As they nod in agreement, Allison continues, "I want to thank both of you for your willingness to come together in the best interest of Carlos. He is a very delightful and intelligent young man. We all care about him and his future. Thank you for your willingness to hear each other's viewpoint." She stands and shakes hands with each of them, while smiling sincerely and making eye contact.

Since conflict is part of the daily life of school leaders, it is imperative to strengthen your skills in building common ground. By mindfully staying calm and centered, you can better understand differences and focus on agreed-on outcomes and common solutions.

Gratitude

Great school leaders spend time strengthening relationships with those they serve. These leaders continually work to build a culture where people feel valued and appreciated.

One of the greatest ways mindful school leaders can instill joy and peace for those they serve is through showing *gratitude*. Gratitude has three components: (1) warm appreciation, (2) goodwill toward the person or people for whom you are grateful, and (3) a disposition to act from your appreciation (Fitzgerald, 1998). Becoming mindful of ways to show your appreciation can have a great impact on your school culture. When people feel valued and cared for, it often brings out their best. According to a 2013 Glassdoor Team survey, 81 percent of employees would work harder if their boss showed more appreciation. Further, researchers at the University of Pennsylvania and the University of North Carolina found grateful leaders were able to motivate their employees to increase productivity (Grant & Gino, 2010).

When showing gratitude, authenticity is crucial. If you are just going through the motions of showing appreciation, people will sense you are not truly grateful. True gratitude comes from being genuine. Mindful leaders can make gratitude both a natural and systematic part of who they are and what they do. For example, Douglas R. Cotant (2011), the former CEO of Campbell Soup, sent thirty thousand hand-written thank-you notes to his staff members throughout his tenure. This helped to create a culture of gratitude (Cotant, 2011). Not only do these notes of appreciation positively affect the receiver, but also, research shows writing letters of gratitude increases both the sender's life satisfaction and overall happiness (Toepfer, Cichy, & Peters, 2012). You can also cultivate a culture of gratitude by systematically incorporating gratitude in your school.

The following list includes specific strategies to assist you in deepening your gratitude in your work life.

1. End each work day with a gratitude reflection. Take a few minutes to consider the positive things you've witnessed during your day as a school leader. You might challenge yourself to bring to mind ten things you're grateful for within your school. Count each gratitude on your fingers until you reach ten.

2. Write one thank-you letter per day to a staff member, student, or parent for whom you feel genuine gratitude. Be specific in your thanks. For example, you might send a gratitude letter to a student who was "caught" doing something right. I recall an eighth-grade student in a middle school where I was the principal. Each day, she sat at a different table in the lunchroom. Her goal was to make friends with every student in the school. I sent a letter of appreciation to her and also to her parents, letting them know how she was reaching out to every student in the school.

3. Begin staff meetings with a moment of genuine gratitude. In a short statement, share one specific thing for which you are grateful. Give thanks for a staff member's efforts and commitment, for example. It is important here to be aware of those who would not appreciate public praise. It is also important to extend appreciation to those who are not necessarily the standouts.

The following fictional scenario demonstrates one school leader's gratitude practice.

Victor, a high school principal, reflected on what he was grateful for throughout each workday. He divided his gratitude into categories: students, teachers, parents, and support staff. As he reflected, Victor took time to share his gratitude in at least one category every day. Sometimes, his gratitude came in the form of flowers for his office staff. Other times, it was a handwritten note mailed to a student or staff member thanking the person for something specific Victor had noted. In teachers' classrooms, which he frequented often, Victor left sticky notes letting the teachers know the difference they were making in students' lives.

Summary

Mindfulness has the potential to powerfully transform your leadership. This transformation is palpable and can be felt by those you serve. Through practices such as mindful listening, mindful speaking, leading with compassion, and expressing gratitude, you can reach out with mindfulness to lead others with peacefulness, kindness, and grace. The next chapter (page 87) offers a nine-week implementation plan for incorporating mindfulness practices in your home life and leadership.

Reflection Questions

Take a moment to respond to the following reflection questions, either in thought or in writing, before moving on to the next chapter.

1. On a scale of 1 to 10, how would I rate myself as a mindful listener? How can I improve this skill?

2. On a scale of 1 to 10, how would I rate myself as a mindful speaker? How can I improve this skill?

3. In what ways do I demonstrate compassion as a leader? When could I incorporate metta meditation to increase my level of compassion?

4. Does my staff know how much I appreciate them? In what ways could I demonstrate authentic gratitude toward them?

5. How could I improve my skills in finding common ground by incorporating mindful leadership?

CHAPTER 4

Enacting the Nine-Week Mindfulness Implementation Plan

eveloping or strengthening your mindfulness practice takes motivation and commitment. To have a high degree of mindfulness, self-discipline and continuity are key. Mindfulness training can be likened to weightlifting: you won't garner results from doing it only once or twice when you're in the mood. As Kabat-Zinn (2013) tells his patients, "You don't have to like it; you just have to do it" (p. 33). Carving out time for mindfulness and mindful meditation may require revamping your schedule and priorities, which is why this chapter provides an implementation plan to help you put your learning from the previous chapters into practice.

The mindfulness implementation plan occurs over nine weeks. For each week, you will discover a figure featuring varied mindfulness practices to work on and recommendations for when and where to implement these practices. The figures also provide space for you to write down, at the end of each week, your commitment to honoring the practices and to reflect on how the practices helped you in your home and work lives. Each week begins fresh with a new plan to follow; there is no need to add the new week's tasks on top of the previous week's. If you prefer to have hard copies of the weekly figures, visit **MarzanoResources.com/reproducibles** to download free reproducible versions of each figure to print out and keep in your home or office.

The implementation plan begins in week one by introducing or reminding you of the importance of both using the breath as an anchor and incorporating silence into your life. The next eight weeks assemble a meditation plan, gradually building on the time commitment required each week. As with this book, the sequence of practices begins with those focused on yourself (weeks one through six) and moves to those that involve reaching out to others (weeks seven through nine).

Before you begin, it is also helpful to have a vision of what you want to cultivate through your mindfulness and mindful meditation practices. Create a vision of your best possible self as a school leader (later, you can extend this by considering a vision of your best self as a spouse, parent, or friend). According to Kabat-Zinn (2013), "Your vision should be what you believe is most fundamental to your ability to be your best self, to be at peace with yourself, to be fully integrated as a person, to be whole" (p. 38).

The implementation plan directs you to practice mindfulness techniques according to certain time limits each week. This enables you to easily begin these practices, even as a mindfulness beginner. Please keep in mind that the recommendations for time limits or when to practice the mindfulness exercises are simply suggestions. Most important is that you find and stick to what works within your schedule. I encourage you to use this plan as a guide or map rather than something else on your to-do list.

Week One: Mindful Breathing and Intentional Silence

As you embark on your mindfulness implementation plan, you should *begin within*, starting with your breath. Breathing is an anchor for numerous mindfulness practices. It anchors you to the present moment, bringing you back to the here and now. With this anchor, you will be better equipped to handle the stresses of day-to-day life.

This first week of practice also includes time for intentional silence. Intentional silence can help you bring a sense of peace and calmness to your home and work lives. At first, intentional silence can seem quite uncomfortable, but with time and intentionality, you can experience the peaceful benefits of silence.

Figure 4.1 describes the mindfulness practices for week one.

Mindfulness Practice	Recommendation	Your Personal Commitment	Reflection
Belly breathing (see page 37) for five breaths	Once a day for the first two days, at home or in a quiet, safe space Then once a day for five or more days in the school setting	I commit to practicing belly breathing in the following manner:	What I learned:
Box breathing (see page 38) for five repetitions	Once a day for three or more days, at home or in a quiet, safe space Then once a day for two or more days in the school setting	I commit to practicing box breathing in the following manner:	What I learned:
Intentional silence (see page 40) for ten minutes	Once a day for two or more days, at home or in a quiet, safe space	I commit to practicing intentional silence in the following manner:	What I learned:

FIGURE 4.1: Mindfulness practices—week one.

*Visit **MarzanoResources.com/reproducibles** to download a free reproducible version of this figure.*

Week Two: Mindful Meditation

Having practiced both using your breath as an anchor and intentional silence, you have set the groundwork for beginning or strengthening a mindful meditation practice. Before beginning this week's practice, spend some time selecting a space for your meditation. This should be a warm, comfortable, quiet space where others will not interrupt you. Also, I recommend you download a meditation app that tracks both the time and the consecutive days you practice meditation. Choices of both free and paid apps are available in the appendix (page 101).

Figure 4.2 describes the mindfulness practices for week two.

Mindfulness Practice	Recommendation	Your Personal Commitment	Reflection
Mindful meditation (see page 42) for five minutes for beginners and ten or more minutes for advanced practitioners	Once a day every day, either first thing in the morning or as you end your day	I commit to practicing mindful meditation in the following manner:	What I learned:

FIGURE 4.2: Mindfulness practices—week two.

*Visit **MarzanoResources.com/reproducibles** to download a free reproducible version of this figure.*

Week Three: Daily Intention Setting and Mindful Meditation

Setting intentions is a powerful mindfulness practice to help you focus on what matters to you most. Serving as a *North Star* (or your personal mission statement), intention setting helps you show up with purpose in both your home and work lives. It helps you live with intentionality in accordance with your values. Even difficult conversations can be opportunities in which to intentionally practice courage and kindness.

I recommend you set daily intentions first thing in the morning to serve as a rudder for your day. This one mindfulness practice can truly be life changing. During the week, I also recommend growing your daily meditation practice. As you continue your daily meditation, you may ask yourself, "Am I doing this right?" You may find yourself lost in thought, which is perfectly normal. Minds think! As you become aware you are thinking, gently bring yourself back to your breath. Continue this process throughout your sitting practice. Some days you may find yourself extremely calm and focused; other days, you may be less so. Either way, you are still meditating correctly. Praise yourself for your dedication to the practice.

Figure 4.3 describes the mindfulness practices for week three.

Mindfulness Practice	Recommendation	Your Personal Commitment	Reflection
Daily intention setting (see page 46) for three to five minutes	Once a day for two days, first thing in the morning, setting intentions concerning your home life Once a day for two days, first thing in the morning, setting intentions concerning your work life	I commit to setting intentions for the day in the following manner:	What I learned:
Mindful meditation (see page 42) for seven minutes for beginners and thirteen or more minutes for advanced practitioners	Once a day every day, either first thing in the morning or as you end your day	I commit to practicing mindful meditation in the following manner:	What I am learning from meditation:

FIGURE 4.3: Mindfulness practices—week three.

*Visit **MarzanoResources.com/reproducibles** to download a free reproducible version of this figure.*

Week Four: Unplugging and Mindful Meditation

Unplugging from technology is beneficial for both your overall well-being and that of those you serve. Although unplugging at work can be difficult (due to others' needs to contact you in case of emergencies, concerns, and conflicts), there are still steps you can take to balance the impact technology has on your life. In week four, I encourage you to set personal goals to limit technology in your home and in the school setting.

I also recommend furthering your meditation practice. As you continue with your mindful meditation, know the results are not always apparent—at first. I recommend you continue your daily meditation practice. Even if you can only commit to a few minutes, this consistency provides the most benefits. Although the time commitment for mindful meditation is not increased in week four, feel free to add additional time to your practice. If you are finding it relatively easy to meet the time commitment and you are not struggling with the meditation practice (physically or mentally), experiment with adding more time and adjusting as needed.

Figure 4.4 describes the mindfulness practices for week four.

Mindfulness Practice	Recommendation	Your Personal Commitment	Reflection
Unplugging (see page 48) at home and school	One personal goal for limiting technology at home and school	I commit to unplugging at home in the following manner: I commit to unplugging at work in the following manner:	What I learned:
Mindful meditation (see page 42) for seven minutes for beginners and thirteen or more minutes for advanced practitioners	Once a day, first thing in the morning or as you end your day	I commit to practicing mindful meditation in the following manner:	What I learned:

FIGURE 4.4: Mindfulness practices—week four.

*Visit **MarzanoResources.com/reproducibles** to download a free reproducible version of this figure.*

Week Five: Self-Compassion and Mindful Meditation

In the hectic world of school leadership, where something will go wrong eventually, leaders often tend to dwell on self-criticism. Practicing self-compassion is an activity that helps you learn to be a good friend to yourself. Further, it provides you with more compassion and empathy to give to those you serve.

During week five, I recommend continuing to sit and meditate daily. If you find yourself becoming fidgety, take a moment to calm yourself. Imagine yourself sitting still like a rock—don't move. If you feel any part of your body itching, try to avoid scratching by focusing on stillness. Make a commitment to be still. If you feel antsy, you can choose to make that your focus for meditation. Simply notice your feeling of restlessness. Breathe into it, but do not move your body. With some practice, you will be able to sit still for longer periods of time. Find a place between being alert and relaxed. Over time, this will bring an inner sense of peace and stillness.

Figure 4.5 describes mindfulness practices for week five.

Mindfulness Practice	Recommendation	Your Personal Commitment	Reflection
Self-compassion (see page 53)	Twice during the week, for three to four minutes each time	I commit to practicing self-compassion in the following manner:	What I learned:
Mindful meditation (see page 42) for seven minutes for beginners and thirteen or more minutes for advanced practitioners	Once a day, first thing in the morning or as you end your day	I commit to practicing mindful meditation in the following manner:	What I learned:

FIGURE 4.5: Mindfulness practices—week five.

*Visit **MarzanoResources.com/reproducibles** to download a free reproducible version of this figure.*

Week Six: Mindful Listening and Mindful Meditation

As you enter week six of your practice, turn your attention to reaching out mindfully, beginning with mindful listening. Listening with full presence is a tremendous gift you give to those you serve and love. By setting your own thoughts and views aside, you can learn to embody receptivity.

During week six, I recommend lengthening your mindful meditation to the number of minutes with which you feel comfortable. In figure 4.6, I recommend ten minutes for beginners and sixteen minutes for more advanced practitioners. If this is too easy or too difficult, feel free to adjust the time to your needs. Longer sitting periods provide the opportunity for a deeper stillness and greater self-awareness. As you determine the amount of time you will dedicate to your sitting practice, aim for the sweet spot that feels slightly challenging but not demotivating. The important thing is to maintain your daily practice.

Figure 4.6 describes the mindfulness practices for week six.

Mindfulness Practice	Recommendation	Your Personal Commitment	Reflection
Mindful listening (see page 68)	Once at home and once at work	I commit to mindful listening in the following manner:	What I learned:
Mindful meditation (see page 42) for ten minutes for beginners and sixteen or more minutes for advanced practitioners	Once a day, first thing in the morning or as you end your day	I commit to practicing mindful meditation in the following manner:	What I learned:

FIGURE 4.6: Mindfulness practices—week six.

*Visit **MarzanoResources.com/reproducibles** to download a free reproducible version of this figure.*

Week Seven: Mindful Speaking and Mindful Meditation

After practicing mindful listening in week six, this week you will turn your attention to mindful speaking. Your speech reflects your inner self. By paying closer attention to your intention and being aware of your audience's needs, you can be more thoughtful with your words.

As you continue your mindful meditation practice, it is important to have patience. Results do not happen overnight. Over time and with consistency, you may experience numerous benefits, including decreased anxiety, an improved outlook on life, and a stronger understanding of yourself. I encourage you to stay with your sitting practice.

Figure 4.7 describes the mindfulness practices for week seven.

Mindfulness Practice	Recommendation	Your Personal Commitment	Reflection
Mindful speaking (see page 72)	Once at home and once at work	I commit to practicing mindful speaking in the following manner:	What I learned:
Mindful meditation (see page 42) for ten minutes for beginners and sixteen or more minutes for advanced practitioners	Once a day, first thing in the morning or as you end your day	I commit to practicing mindful meditation in the following manner:	What I learned:

FIGURE 4.7: Mindfulness practices—week seven.

*Visit **MarzanoResources.com/reproducibles** to download a free reproducible version of this figure.*

Week Eight: Leading With Compassion and Mindful Meditation

Whether you are dealing with a parent who is upset, a teacher who is hurting, or a student who is being bullied, leading with compassion helps people deal with their frustrations, fears, and anger. A powerful practice for deepening compassion is the ancient practice of metta meditation, also known as *loving-kindness meditation*. This is the focus of week eight.

I also recommend further meditation. As you continue to strengthen your mindful meditation practice, you may want to consider sitting each day at the same time, in the same space. To make this a lasting habit, consistency is key. If this is not always possible, keep in mind that you can meditate anytime, anywhere. If you miss meditating for a day or two, take note of your reasons so in the future, you can find ways to commit even more fully to the practice.

Figure 4.8 describes the mindfulness practices for week eight.

Mindfulness Practice	Recommendation	Your Personal Commitment	Reflection
Compassionate leadership (see page 64)	Metta meditation twice during the week	I commit to practicing metta meditation in the following manner:	What I learned:
Mindful meditation (see page 42) for twelve minutes for beginners and eighteen or more minutes for advanced practitioners	Once a day, first thing in the morning or as you end your day	I commit to practicing mindful meditation in the following manner:	What I learned:

FIGURE 4.8: Mindfulness practices—week eight.

*Visit **MarzanoResources.com/reproducibles** to download a free reproducible version of this figure.*

Week Nine: Gratitude and Mindful Meditation

When you look for the good in others, it can bring out their best. Gratitude increases joy and well-being in those who receive it *and* give it. Therefore, being mindful of showing gratitude toward those you serve can greatly influence your school culture.

In your meditation practice, you may find yourself judging your meditation as either good or bad. However, you should not judge the process of meditation. Rather, try adopting an attitude of non-judgment by simply *being* during your meditation and accepting whatever arises in the present moment. Sometimes this will feel like a great sense of calmness, and peace overcomes you. Other times it will feel like time spent making lists. Both are normal for even the most seasoned meditators.

Figure 4.9 describes the mindfulness practices for week nine.

Mindfulness Practice	Recommendation	Your Personal Commitment	Reflection
Gratitude (see page 84)	One letter of gratitude each workday, being specific in your thanks	I commit to practicing gratitude in the following manner:	What I learned:
Mindful meditation (see page 42) for thirteen minutes for beginners and twenty or more minutes for advanced practitioners	Once a day, first thing in the morning or as you end your day	I commit to practicing mindful meditation in the following manner:	What I learned:

FIGURE 4.9: Mindfulness practices—week nine.

Visit MarzanoResources.com/reproducibles to download a free reproducible version of this figure.

Beyond Week Nine

As you conclude the nine-week implementation plan, use figure 4.10 to consider how you will continue to make mindful meditation and other mindfulness practices part of your daily life at school and home. I recommend you maintain a consistent, daily meditation practice and continue to weave other mindfulness practices into your life.

When I first began my mindfulness practice in the early 1990s, I often had my two-year-old sitting on my lap during my meditation time! I soon learned to set my alarm thirty minutes earlier than the rest of my family so I could settle into a more focused meditation each morning. To maintain a consistent practice, I only allow myself a cup of coffee *after* my meditation. It's what works for me.

Sometimes when my routine is jumbled due to vacations or holidays, I unintentionally miss a meditation. To overcome this, I try to mentally plan ahead for how mindfulness can fit into these varied schedules. As of this writing, I have meditated 444 days in a row, and have implemented many mindfulness strategies into my daily routines. For example, my daughter and I text each other a specific gratitude every evening. Before I meet with friends or colleagues, I make a mental note to speak mindfully. My goal—although I don't always achieve it—is to make sure my words add positivity and goodwill. When I find myself in the web of being self-critical or critical of others, I take the time to practice metta meditation. When I am stressed at work, I pause and practice box breathing. My husband and I eat dinner mindfully every evening we're together. The television is off. Technology is out of sight. The table is set. The candle is lit. We take time to enjoy the food and conversation. Even when our children were young, this was our practice. These are just a few of the examples of how mindfulness is part of my everyday life.

My Commitment to Continue Implementing Mindfulness Practices at Home	My Commitment to Implementing Mindfulness Practices at School	My Commitment to Incorporating Meditation in My Daily Life

FIGURE 4.10: Ongoing mindfulness practices.

*Visit **MarzanoResources.com/reproducibles** to download a free reproducible version of this figure.*

Summary

In this section, you received a nine-week implementation plan for incorporating mindfulness into your life. I also discussed ways you might continue to implement mindfulness practices into your personal and professional lives. Although this concludes the subject matter for the book, the appendix (page 101) provides additional recommended resources to assist you on your mindfulness journey, should you wish to read further.

On a personal note, I want to thank you for your dedication to developing your mindfulness practice. My wish is that it helps you to continue to lead with excellence, clarity, focus, and love. Your leadership touches so many lives. Your presence is powerful. May you find peacefulness through your mindful leadership practice.

Reflection Questions

Take a moment to respond to the following reflection questions, either in thought or in writing, as you conclude this book.

1. What is the vision I want to cultivate through my mindfulness and meditation practices?

2. How can I consistently include mindfulness practices in my home life, even when I don't feel like it?

3. How can I consistently include mindfulness practices in my work life, even when I don't feel like it?

Appendix

Recommended Resources

Here you will find a list of recommended apps, books, magazines, and websites to help you continue to develop your skills in mindfulness and mindful leadership.

Apps

Meditation and mindfulness apps offer a variety of meditations and courses to help you decrease your stress and anxiety. Several offer timers and tracking devices to assist you in strengthening your mindfulness and meditation practice. With the many apps available, it is important to consider the app that's ideal for your skill level, budget, and tracking needs. You might also consider other features many apps include, such as videos, music, and tutorials, which might best support your practice. Following are some recommended apps.

- *Calm* **(Smith & Tew, 2022).** This paid app is popular for de-stressing and improving sleep. It offers meditations of varying lengths, music, relaxing stories, as well as a thirty-day meditation training for beginners. *Calm* includes video lessons on mindful movement and stretching. It also offers trainings on mindfulness, meditation, and other relevant topics.

- *Headspace: Mindful Meditation* (**Puddicombe & Pierson, 2022**). This popular paid app is appealing because of its variety of meditations for all levels and a ten-day beginners' guide with daily guided meditations in an easy-to-use, attractive format. *Headspace* tracks how many minutes and days you've meditated and offers a mindfulness quote each day. It also includes a library of informational topics, such as relationships, anxiety, performance, and sleep.

- *Healthy Minds Program* (**Davidson, 2022**). Rife with easy-to-complete lessons and meditations, the goal of the *Healthy Minds Program* is to improve overall well-being. This free app is structured into four pillars for training the mind: (1) awareness, (2) connection, (3) insight, and (4) purpose. It also offers a collection of twenty-seven meditations.

- *Insight Timer* (**Plowman & Plowman, 2022**). This free meditation app offers 130 thousand guided meditations. It also includes a vast selection of audio tracks and a variety of meditation types (mindfulness, children's, walking, sleeping, breathing, and transcendental). With *Insight Timer*, you can easily monitor how many consecutive days you have meditated. Both *Time* and *Women's Health* magazines named *Insight Timer* an app of the year (as cited in Yates, 2022). This app offers access to well-known meditation and spirituality teachers, as well as the ability to download meditations to listen to offline.

- *Optimize by Heroic* (**Heroic Enterprises, 2022**). Although not a meditation or mindfulness app, *Optimize by Heroic* is a free app offering over six hundred Philosophers Notes, which are six-page excerpts (in PDF form) from books about optimal living. It also includes over fifty master classes on topics such as positive psychology, sleep, leadership, meditation, and peak performance, which promote more wisdom in less time.

- *Smiling Mind* (**Martino & Tutton, 2022**). This free app offers programs such as stress management, mindful foundations, and sleep. It is easy to navigate between programs to find the right fit for you.

Psychologists and educators created and originally designed this app for children, but it now offers numerous mindfulness sessions for both children and adults. Pertinent to school leaders are eight sessions to help you digitally detox, as well as ten sessions related to stress management. It also offers hundreds of meditations lasting from five to forty-five minutes. The app includes programs interspersed with meditations, such as a journaling activity.

- *UCLA Mindful* (**UCLA Mindful Awareness Research Center, 2022**). This is a free app ideal for those new to meditation. It includes a Getting Started section with information on posture, mindfulness research, and how to select meditations right for you. It offers a meditation timer, as well as weekly thirty-minute meditations on varied mindfulness themes. For those suffering from health issues, *UCLA Mindful* offers wellness meditations. This app is available in both English and Spanish.

Books and Magazines

There are numerous books and magazines about mindfulness, meditation, and leadership. The following are those I recommend as most relevant to mindful school leaders.

- *Buddha's Brain: The Practical Neuroscience of Happiness, Love, & Wisdom* (**Hanson, 2009**). A senior neurologist, clinical psychologist, and meditation teacher wrote this book, which provides highly practical tools, practices, and guided meditations to help people literally rewire their brains. The author shares research about mindfulness to help readers strengthen positive brain states to have deeper relaxation, happiness, and wisdom. He encourages readers to make a commitment to never miss a day of meditation.

- *The Leadership Challenge: How to Make Extraordinary Things Happen in Organizations* (**Kouzes & Posner, 2012**). A valuable resource for all school leaders, this book shares how leadership is a skill school leaders can learn and hone. Based on the research of the coauthors, it offers examples and case studies of excellence in leadership.

- *Lead Yourself First: Inspiring Leadership Through Solitude* **(Kethledge & Irwin, 2017).** By exploring the relationship between solitude and leadership, this book guides leaders to understand the importance of solitude and how to obtain it. The authors discuss how solitude can improve one's clarity, emotional balance, and courage. It includes historical depictions of leaders such as Martin Luther King Jr. and Winston Churchill, who both relied on solitude during the conflicts and trials of leadership.

- *Planet Mindful* **magazine by Anthem (https://anthem.co.uk /our-brands/wellbeing/planet-mindful).** This colorful, well-written magazine offers up-to-date mindfulness articles based on the latest science. Each month is based on a theme, such as resilience, self-care, the science of mindfulness, and loving-kindness.

- *Mindfulness: An Eight-Week Plan for Finding Peace in a Frantic World* **(Williams & Penman, 2011).** This book offers easy-to-do mindfulness strategies to assist you in releasing stress and finding a sense of peace and calmness. Based on mindfulness-based cognitive therapy (MBCT) and other scientifically grounded strategies, this book provides an eight-week program you can implement in ten to twenty minutes per day. It includes both written descriptions and links to audio meditations.

- *The Mindful School Leader: Practices to Transform Your Leadership and School* **(Brown & Olson, 2015).** Offering profiles of mindful school leaders, this inspirational book provides tools and strategies for incorporating mindfulness into your daily leadership practices. It is rife with practical applications for deepening your mindful leadership skills.

- *The Miracle of Mindfulness: An Introduction Into the Practice of Meditation* **(Hanh, 1999).** A Vietnamese Buddhist Zen master wrote this book to teach readers how to be more fully awake and aware through their mindfulness practice. The author explores what constitutes a miracle and explains to his readers that "all is a miracle" (p. 12). He guides the reader in understanding how mindfulness can restore wholeness in every moment of your life. Originally, the author wrote this book as a lengthy letter to a staff member in South Vietnam to encourage him to continue with engaged Buddhism.

- *Why Meditate: Working With Thoughts and Emotions* (**Ricard, 2010**). This thoughtful book explains the many benefits of meditation and how to do it. The author, a Buddhist monk, writes about the theory, scientific evidence, and spirituality of meditation. For those new to understanding the *why* and *how* of meditation, this is a must-read.

- *Wherever You Go, There You Are: Mindfulness Meditation in Everyday Life* (**Kabat-Zinn, 1994**). Through a collection of thoughts and stories, a professor of medicine at the University of Massachusetts guides readers into a deeper understanding of mindful meditation. He overviews the numerous health benefits that result from integrating mindful meditation into your life, helping you develop a clear *why* for developing and sustaining the practice. The book has short, manageable chapters written in a clear style. This book has become a classic for those interested in mindfulness.

Websites

Various websites provide insights, articles, tips, and inspiration to help people live and lead more mindfully. I recommend the following three top sites.

- *Mindful.org* (**www.mindful.org**). This free site is a fit for both beginners and seasoned mindful practitioners. It offers personal stories, mindfulness articles, and science that help bring mindfulness into the mainstream. It includes a tutorial on how to meditate, ideas to focus your mindfulness, ways to bring more compassion into your life and strengthen your ability to be calm, and strategies for dealing with anxiety.

- *Mindful Leader* (**www.mindfulleader.org**). This website's mission is "to create mindful and compassionate work environments." It offers mindfulness leadership training, including silent meditation retreats, an eight-week course in mindfulness-based stress reduction, mindful leader summits, and certification programs. The website also provides free online Meditate Together opportunities via Zoom five days a week, twenty-four hours a day. There is a free email subscription for the latest tips and tools, as well as information of upcoming mindfulness events.

- *Palouse Mindfulness* (**https://palousemindfulness.com**). This free site offers an online Mindfulness-Based Stress-Reduction training course certified Mindfulness-Based Stress Reduction instructor Dave Potter designed. This training, taking you through numerous mindfulness-based practices, is an eight-week course based on the program Jon Kabat-Zinn founded. It includes videos by renowned mindfulness teachers, including Kabat-Zinn, Thich Nhat Hanh, Sharon Salzberg, and Kristin Neff.

References and Resources

Arendt, J. F. W., Verdorfer, A. P., & Kugler, K. G. (2019). Mindfulness and leadership: Communication as a behavioral correlate of leader mindfulness and its effect on follower satisfaction. *Frontiers in Psychology, 10,* 667.

Basso, J. C., McHale, A., Ende, V., Oberlin, D. J., & Suzuki, W. A. (2019). Brief, daily meditation enhances attention, memory, mood, and emotional regulation in non-experienced meditators. *Behavioural Brain Research, 356,* 208–220.

Bender, D. (n.d.). *Tips to incorporate mindful breaks from technology* [Blog post]. Accessed at https://blog.nasm.org/fitness/tips-to-incorporate-mindful-breaks-from-technology on June 21, 2022.

Bernardi, L., Porta, C., & Sleight, P. (2006). Cardiovascular, cerebrovascular, and respiratory changes induced by different types of music in musicians and non-musicians: The importance of silence. *Heart, 92*(4), 445–452.

Bertin, M. (2017, July 17). *A daily mindful walking practice: Take a break and boost your mood with this 10-minute walking meditation.* Accessed at www.mindful.org/daily-mindful-walking-practice on September 13, 2022.

Bhatta, K. (2019). *Journey from life to life: Achieving higher purpose.* Ladera Ranch, CA: Redwood.

Biegel, G. M., Brown, K. W., Shapiro, S. L., & Schubert, C. M. (2009). Mindfulness-based stress reduction for the treatment of adolescent psychiatric outpatients: A randomized clinical trial. *Journal of Consulting and Clinical Psychology, 77*(5), 855–866.

Block-Lerner, J., Adair, C., Plumb, J. C., Rhatigan, D. L., & Orsillo, S. M. (2007). The case for mindfulness-based approaches in the cultivation of empathy: Does nonjudgmental, present-moment awareness increase capacity for perspective-taking and empathic concern? *Journal of Marital and Family Therapy, 33*(4), 501–516.

Bostock, S., Crosswell, A. D., Prather, A. A., & Steptoe, A. (2019). Mindfulness on-the-go: Effects of a mindfulness meditation app on work stress and well-being. *Journal of Occupational Health Psychology, 24*(1), 127–138.

Bradley, C. (2018). *The power of pause: Discover how to up your game and perform your best.* Accessed at www.mindful.org/the-power-of-pause on June 22, 2022.

Branstrom, R., Kvillemo, P., Brandberg, Y., & Moskowitz, J. T. (2010). Self-report mindfulness as a mediator of psychological well-being in a stress reduction intervention for cancer patients—A randomized study. *Annals of Behavioral Medicine, 39*(2), 151–161.

Breines, J. G., & Chen, S. (2012). Self-compassion increases self-improvement motivation. *Personality and Social Psychology Bulletin, 38*(9), 113–114.

Broderick, P. C. (2005). Mindfulness and coping with dysphoric mood: Contrasts with rumination and distraction. *Cognitive Therapy and Research, 29*, 501–510.

Brown, V., & Olson, K. (2015). *The mindful school leader: Practices to transform your leadership and school.* Thousand Oaks, CA: Corwin.

Carmichael, C. (2021). *Nervous energy: Harness the power of your anxiety.* New York: St. Martin's Essentials.

Carter, J. (2022, January 31). *Compassionate leadership: How to do hard things in a human way.* Accessed at https://hbr.org/webinar/2021/12/compassionate-leadership-how-to-do-hard-things-in-a-human-way on June 22, 2022.

Cassata, C. (2021, June 8). *10 areas that mindfulness and meditation make us better* [Blog post]. Accessed at https://psychcentral.com/blog/surprising-health -benefits-of-mindfulness-meditation on September 30, 2022.

Catherine, S. (2008). *Focused and fearless: A meditator's guide to states of deep joy, calm, and clarity*. Somerville, MA: Wisdom.

Chambers, R., Gullone, E., & Allen, N. B. (2009). Mindful emotion regulation: An integrative review. *Clinical Psychology Review, 29*(6), 560–572.

Chambers, R., Lo, B. C. Y., & Allen, N. B. (2008). The impact of intensive mindfulness training on attentional control, cognitive style, and affect. *Cognitive Therapy and Research, 32*(3), 303–322.

Charoensukmongkol, P. (2014). Benefits of mindfulness meditation on emotional intelligence, general self-efficacy, and perceived stress: Evidence from Thailand. *Journal of Spirituality in Mental Health, 16*(3), 171–192.

Chiesa, A., & Serretti, A. (2009). Mindfulness-based stress reduction for stress management in healthy people: A review and meta-analysis. *Journal of Alternative and Complementary Medicine, 15*(5), 593–600.

Chowdhury, M. R. (2019, July 27). What is loving-kindness meditation? *Positive Psychology*. Accessed at https://positivepsychology.com/loving-kindness -meditation on September 30, 2022.

Christakis, D. (2011, December 28). *Media and children* [Video file]. Accessed at www.youtube.com/watch?v=BoT7qH_uVNo on June 22, 2022.

Cohen, J. S., & Miller, L. J. (2009). Interpersonal mindfulness training for well-being: A pilot study with psychology graduate students. *Teachers College Record, 111*(12), 2760–2774.

Cotant, D. R. (2011, February 16). *Secrets of positive feedback*. Accessed at https://hbr.org/2011/02/secrets-of-positive-feedback on June 22, 2022.

Covey, S. R. (2020). *The 7 habits of highly effective people* (Rev. & updated ed.). New York: Simon & Schuster.

Curtin, E. (2014, February 21). *Feeling good yet? Seven ways to boost endorphins* [Blog post]. Accessed at https://goodtherapy.org/blog/feeling-good-yet -seven-ways-to-boost-endorphins on September 15, 2022.

Daskal, L. (n.d.). *10 ways meditation can make you a better leader*. Accessed at www.lollydaskal.com/leadership/10-ways-meditation-can-make-you-a -better-leader on October 3, 2022.

Davidson, R. (2022). *Healthy minds program* [Mobile app]. Google Play Store. Accessed at https://play.google.com/store/apps/details?id=com.healthy minds&hl=en_US&gl=US on September 30, 2022.

DeWitt, P. (2020, October 24). *School leaders were asked about their stress levels. Here's what they told us* [Blog post]. Accessed at www.edweek.org /leadership/opinion-school-leaders-were-asked-about-their-stress-levels -heres-what-they-told-us/2020/12 on June 22, 2022.

Diwanji, K. (2019, April 7). Why leaders need to be mindful in this VUCA world? *LinkedIn.* Accessed at https://linkedin.com/pulse/why-leaders-need -mindful-vuca-world-kala-diwanji#:~:text=As%20Buddhist%20monk%20 Thich%20Nhat,passion%2C%20compassion%20and%20courage%20 reside on October 5, 2022.

Drinko, C. (2021, August 4). *We're worse at listening than we realize* [Blog post]. Accessed at www.psychologytoday.com/us/blog/play-your-way -sane/202108/were-worse-listening-we-realize on October 3, 2022.

Duffy, M. K., Ganster, D. C., & Pagon, M. (2002). Social undermining in the workplace. *Academy of Management Journal, 45*(2), 331–351.

Duke Human Resources. (n.d.). *Breathing for relaxation.* Accessed at https://hr.duke.edu/wellness/mental-health-stress/success-over-stress /relaxation-techniques/breathing-relaxation on September 30, 2022.

Edwards, M. K., Rosenbaum S., & Loprinzi, P. D. (2018). Differential experimental effects of a short bout of walking, meditation, or combination of walking and meditation on state anxiety among young adults. *American Journal of Health Promotion, 32*(4), 949–958.

Fitzgerald, P. (1998). Gratitude and justice. *Ethics, 109*(1), 119–153.

Fletcher, J. (2022, June 16). *How to practice mindful listening.* Accessed at https://psychcentral.com/lib/mindful-listening-exercise on October 3, 2022.

Fox, K. C., Nijeboer, S., Dixon, M. L., Floman, J. L., Ellamil, M., Rumak, S. P., et al. (2014). Is meditation associated with altered brain structure? A systematic review and meta-analysis of morphometric neuroimaging in meditation practitioners. *Neuroscience and Biobehavioral Reviews, 43*, 48–73.

Fronsdal, G. (2022). *Mindful speaking*. Accessed at www.insightmeditationcenter
.org/books-articles/mindful-speaking on June 22, 2022.

Fullan, M. (2020). *Leading in a culture of change* (2nd ed.). San
Francisco: Jossey-Bass.

Gensler, E. (Host). (2021, May). CI to eye: Inside Google's employee mindfulness
program: Nik Rama [Audio podcast episode]. In *CI to Eye*. Accessed at
https://open.spotify.com/episode/6VZco2XDJhWwWYQLSHFbma on
October 7, 2022.

Geschwind, N., Peeters, F., Drukker, M., van Os, J., & Wichers, M. (2011).
Mindfulness training increases momentary positive emotions and reward
experience in adults vulnerable to depression: A randomized controlled
trial. *Journal of Consulting and Clinical Psychology, 79*(5), 618–628.

Gilbert, P. (2009). *The compassionate mind: A new approach to life's challenges.*
Oakland, CA: New Harbinger.

Giluk, T. L. (2010). *Mindfulness-based stress reduction: Facilitating work outcomes
through experienced affect and high-quality relationships* [Doctoral
dissertation, University of Iowa]. Iowa Research Online. Accessed at
https://iro.uiowa.edu/esploro/outputs/doctoral/Mindfulness-based-stress
-reduction-facilitating-work-outcomes/9983777116902771 on
June 22, 2022.

Glassdoor Team. (2013, November 13). *Employees to retain half of their employees
longer if bosses showed more appreciation* [Blog post]. Accessed at
www.glassdoor.com/employers/blog/employers-to-retain-half-of-their
-employees-longer-if-bosses-showed-more-appreciation-glassdoor-survey on
June 22, 2022.

Glomb, T. M., Duffy, M. K., Bono, J. E., & Yang, T. (2012). Mindfulness at work.
Research in Personnel and Human Resources Management, 30, 115–157.

Goguen-Hughes, L. (2011, January 26). *Aetna employees being mindful: The business
world is catching on to the benefits of mindfulness, and Aetna's now on
board.* Accessed at www.mindful.org/aetna-employees-being-mindful on
September 26, 2022.

Goldin, P. R., & Gross, J. J. (2010). Effects of Mindfulness-Based Stress Reduction
(MBSR) on emotion regulation in social anxiety disorder. *Emotion,
10*(1), 83–91.

Goldstein, E. D. (2007). Sacred moments: Implications on well-being and stress. *Journal of Clinical Psychology, 63*(10), 1001–1019.

Goleman, D. (1995). *Emotional intelligence.* New York: Bantam Books.

Goodreads. (n.d.). *Martin Luther King Jr. quotes.* Accessed at: https://goodreads .com/quotes/68713-a-genuine-leader-is-not-a-searcher-for-consensus-but on October 3, 2022.

Grant, A. M., & Gino, F. (2010). A little thanks goes a long way: Explaining why gratitude expressions motivate prosocial behavior. *Journal of Personality and Social Psychology, 98*(6), 946–955.

Guendelman, S., Medeiros, S., & Rampes, H. (2017). Mindfulness and emotion regulation: Insights from neurobiological psychological and clinical studies. *Frontiers in Psychology, 8*, 220.

Guglietti C. L., Daskalakis, Z. J., Radhu, N., Fitzgerald, P. B., & Ritvo, P. (2013). Meditation-related increases in GABAB modulated cortical inhibition. *Brain Stimulation, 6*(3), 397–402.

Hafenbrack, A.C., Cameron, L. D., Spreitzer, G. M., Zhang, C., Noval, L. J., & Shaffakat, S. (2020). Helping people by being in the present: Mindfulness increases prosocial behavior. *Organizational Behavior and Human Decision Processes, 159*, 21–38.

Halliwell, E. (2020, January 7). *Why mindfulness begins with the breath.* Accessed at www.mindful.org/6-reasons-why-mindfulness-begins-with-the-breath on September 26, 2022.

Hanh, T. N. (1999). *The miracle of mindfulness: An introduction to the practice of meditation.* Boston, MA: Beacon Press.

Hanh, T. N. (2013). *The art of communicating.* New York: HarperCollins.

Hanh, T. N. (2015). *A handful of quiet: Happiness in four pebbles.* Berkeley, CA: Plum Blossom Books.

Hanson, R. (2009). *Buddha's brain: The practical neuroscience of happiness, love & wisdom.* Oakland, CA: New Harbinger.

Hanson, R. (2013). *Hardwiring happiness: The new brain science of contentment, calm, and confidence.* New York: Harmony Books.

Harte, J. L., Eifert, G. H., & Smith, R. (1995). The effects of running and meditation on beta-endorphin, corticotropin-releasing hormone and cortisol in plasma, and on mood. *Biological Psychology, 40*(3), 251–265.

Harter, J. (2020). *COVID-19: What employees need from leaders right now.* Accessed at www.gallup.com/workplace/297497/covid-employees-need-leaders-right .aspx on June 22, 2022.

Heroic Enterprises. (2022). *Optimize by Heroic* [Mobile app]. Google Play Store. Accessed at https://play.google.com/store/apps/details?id=me.optimize&hl =en_US&gl=US on September 30, 2022.

Hofmann, S. G., Sawyer, A. T., Witt A. A., & Oh, D. (2010). The effect of mindfulness-based therapy on anxiety and depression: A meta-analytic review. *Journal of Consulting and Clinical Psychology, 78*(2), 169–183.

Hölzel, B. K., Carmody, J., Vangel, M., Congleton, C., Yerramsetti, S. M., Gard, et al. (2011). Mindfulness practice leads to increases in regional brain gray matter density. *Psychiatry Research, 191*(1), 36–43.

Houlis, A. (2021, December 16). *The power of setting intentions—and how to do it correctly.* Accessed at www.shape.com/lifestyle/mind-and-body/mental -health/how-to-set-intentions on June 22, 2022.

Hülsheger, U. R., Alberts, H. J. E. M., Feinholdt, A., & Lang, J. W. B. (2013). Benefits of mindfulness at work: The role of mindfulness in emotion regulation, emotional exhaustion, and job satisfaction. *The Journal of Applied Psychology, 98*(2), 310–325.

Hunt, M. G., Marx, R., Lipson, C., & Young, J. (2018). No more FOMO: Limiting social media decreases loneliness and depression. *Journal of Social and Clinical Psychology, 37*(10), 751–768.

Hyland, P. K., Lee, R. A., & Mills, M. J. (2015). Mindfulness at work: A new approach to improving individual and organizational performance. *Industrial and Organizational Psychology, 8*(4), 576–602.

Iberlin, J. M. (with Ruyle, M.). (2017). *Cultivating mindfulness in the classroom.* Bloomington, IN: Marzano Resources.

Insight Timer. (n.d.). *Guided meditations for effective leadership.* Accessed at https://insighttimer.com/meditation-topics/leadership/browse/guided on October 3, 2022.

Itani, O. (2010, December 14). *Intentions vs. goals: Why one-word intentions work better than goals and new year resolutions* [Blog post]. Accessed at www.omaritani.com/blog/goals-vs-one-word-intentions on June 23, 2022.

Itzchakov, G., & Kluger, A. N. (2018, May 17). *The power of listening in helping people change.* Accessed at https://hbr.org/2018/05/the-power-of-listening -in-helping-people-change on October 3, 2022.

Jha, A. P., Morrison, A. B., Dainer-Best, J., Parker, S., Rostrup, N., & Stanley, E. A. (2015). Minds "at attention": Mindfulness training curbs attentional lapses in military cohorts. *PLoS ONE, 10*(2), e0116889.

Jha, A. P., Stanley, E. A., Kiyonaga, A., Wong, L., & Gelfand, L. (2010). Examining the protective effects of mindfulness training on working memory capacity and affective experience. *Emotion, 10*(1), 54–64.

Jiménez, J. (2021, July 16). *Compassion vs. empathy: Understanding the difference* [Blog post]. Accessed at www.betterup.com/blog/compassion-vs-empathy on September 26, 2022.

Jones, C. (2022, February 1). *Frustrating, exhausting but worth it: School principals tell what their jobs are like now.* Accessed at https://edsource.org /2022/school-principals-tell-what-their-jobs-are-like-now/666708 on June 23, 2022.

Kabat-Zinn, J. (1994). *Wherever you go there you are: Mindfulness meditation in everyday life.* New York: Hyperion.

Kabat-Zinn, J. (2003). Mindfulness-based interventions in context: Past, present, and future. *Clinical Psychology: Science and Practice, 10*(2), 144–156.

Kabat-Zinn, J. (2005a). Bringing mindfulness to medicine: An interview with Jon Kabat-Zinn, PhD. Interview by Karolyn Gazella. *Advances in Mind-Body Medicine, 21*(2), 22–27.

Kabat-Zinn, J. (2005b). *Coming to our senses: Healing ourselves and the world through mindfulness.* New York: Hyperion.

Kabat-Zinn, J. (2013). *Full catastrophe living: Using the wisdom of your body and mind to face stress, pain, and illness* (Rev. and updated ed.). New York: Bantam Books.

Keng, S-L., Smoski, M. J., & Robins, C. J. (2011). Effects of mindfulness on psychological health: A review of empirical studies. *Clinical Psychology Review, 31*(6), 1041–1056.

Kethledge, R. M., & Erwin, M. S. (2017). *Lead yourself first: Inspiring leadership through solitude.* New York: Bloomsbury USA.

Khramtsova, I., & Glascock, P. (2010). Outcomes of an integrated journaling and mindfulness program on a US university campus. *Revista Psihologie, 56*(3–4), 208–218.

Kirste, I., Nicola, Z., Kronenberg, G., Walker, T. L., Liu, R. C., & Kempermann, G. (2015). Is silence golden? Effects of auditory stimuli and their absence on adult hippocampal neurogenesis. *Brain Structure & Function, 220*(2), 1221–1228.

Knight, R., (2015, January 9.). How to handle difficult conversations at work. *Harvard Business Review.* Accessed at https://hbr.org/2015/01/how-to -handle-difficult-conversations-at-work on December 5, 2022.

Kornfield, J. (2009). *The wise heart: A guide to the universal teachings of Buddhist psychology.* New York: Bantam Books.

Kouzes, J. M., & Posner, B. Z. (2010). *The truth about leadership: The no-fads, heart-of-the matter facts you need to know.* San Francisco: Jossey-Bass.

Kouzes, J. M., & Posner, B. Z. (2012). *The leadership challenge: How to make extraordinary things happen in organizations.* San Francisco: Jossey-Bass.

Ladwig, J. (2013, May 22). Brain can be trained in compassion, study shows. *University of Wisconsin News.* Accessed at https://news.wisc.edu/brain-can -be-trained-in-compassion-study-shows on June 23, 2022.

Laurence, E. (2020, October 1). *Intermittent silence is like the modified push-up of mediation—Here's how to practice it.* Accessed at www.wellandgood.com /intermittent-silence on September 26, 2022.

Leading Effectively Staff. (2021, November 12). *Gratitude at work: How giving thanks will make you a better leader.* Accessed at www.ccl.org/articles /leading-effectively-articles/giving-thanks-will-make-you-a-better-leader on June 23, 2022.

Mager, D. (2019, March 22). *Mindfulness and emotional intelligence: Mindfulness practices can significantly upgrade your internal operating system* [Blog post]. Accessed at www.psychologytoday.com/au/blog/some-assembly -required/201903/mindfulness-and-emotional-intelligence on September 26, 2022.

Mahfouz, J. (2018). Mindfulness training for school administrators: Effects on well-being and leadership. *Journal of Educational Administration, 56*(6), 602–619.

Mahfouz, J., Greenberg, M. T., & Rodriguez, A. (2019, October). *Principals' social and emotional competence: A key factor for creating caring schools* [Issue brief]. Accessed at www.prevention.psu.edu/uploads/files/PSU-Principals -Brief-103119.pdf on June 23, 2022.

Martino, J., & Tutton, J. (2022). *Smiling mind* [Mobile app]. Google Play Store. Accessed at https://play.google.com/store/apps/details?id=com .smilingmind.app&hl=en_US&gl=US on September 30, 2022.

Marturano, J. (2014). *Finding the space to lead: A practical guide to mindful leadership.* New York: Bloomsbury Press.

Marzano, R. J., & Marzano, J. S. (2015). *Managing the inner world of teaching: Emotions, interpretations, and actions.* Bloomington, IN: Marzano Resources.

Marzano, R. J., & Waters, T. (2009). *District leadership that works: Striking the right balance.* Bloomington, IN: Solution Tree Press.

Mateo, A. (2020, September 15). *What is mindful running and how do you do it?* Accessed at www.runnersworld.com/training/a22160937/mindfulness-in -running on June 23, 2022.

Maxwell, J. C. (2010). *Everyone communicates, few connect: What the most effective people do differently.* Nashville, TN: Nelson.

Mayer, J. D., Caruso, D. R., & Salovey, P. (2016). The ability model of emotional intelligence: Principles and updates. *Emotion Review, 8*(4), 290–300.

Mayo Clinic Staff. (2022a, April 29). *Meditation: A simple, fast way to reduce stress.* Accessed at www.mayoclinic.org/tests-procedures/meditation/in-depth /meditation/art-20045858 on September 26, 2022.

Mayo Clinic Staff. (2022b, April 8). *Stress management.* Accessed at www.mayoclinic.org/healthy-lifestyle/stress-management/basics/stress -basics/hlv-20049495 on October 3, 2022.

Mays, R. (2017, August 15). *The NFL's mindfulness movement is spreading.* Accessed at www.theringer.com/nfl/2017/8/15/16150616/mindfulness-training -falcons-colts-49ers-dan-quinn on June 23, 2022.

Mungal, A. S., & Sorenson, R. (2021). *Why stress is linked to health and the principalship: A management perspective.* Accessed at www.tepsa.org /resource/why-stress-is-linked-to-health-and-the-principalship-a -management-perspective on September 26, 2022.

National Association of Secondary School Principals. (2021, December 8). *NAASP survey signals a looming mass exodus of principals from schools.* Accessed at www.nassp.org/news/nassp-survey-signals-a-looming-mass-exodus-of -principals-from-schools on September 28, 2022.

National Policy Board for Educational Administration. (2015). *Professional standards for educational leaders.* Reston, VA: Author. Accessed at www.npbea.org/wp-content/uploads/2017/06/Professional-Standards-for -Educational-Leaders_2015.pdf on June 23, 2022.

Nazish, N. (2019, May 30). *How to de-stress in 5 minutes or less according to a Navy SEAL.* Accessed at www.forbes.com/sites/nomanazish/2019/05/30/how-to -de-stress-in-5-minutes-or-less-according-to-a-navy-seal/?sh=720aed3c3046 on June 23, 2022.

Neff, K. (n.d.). *Self-compassion.* Accessed at https://self-compassion.org/the-three -elements-of-self-compassion-2 on June 23, 2022.

Neff, K. (2015, September 30). *The five myths of self-compassion.* Accessed at https://greatergood.berkeley.edu/article/item/the_five_myths_of_self _compassion on June 23, 2022.

Neff, K., & Germer, C. (2018). *The mindful self-compassion workbook: A proven way to accept yourself, build inner strength, and thrive.* New York: Guilford Press.

Neporent, L. (2014, January 21). *Seattle Seahawks will have the "ohm" team advantage.* Accessed at https://abcnews.go.com/Health/seattle-seahawks -ohm-team-advantage/story?id=21614481 on June 23, 2022.

Newberg, A. B., & Iversen, J. (2003). The neural basis of the complex mental task of meditation: Neurotransmitter and neurochemical considerations. *Medical Hypotheses, 61*(2), 282–291.

Nielsen. (2016, June). *The total audience report: Q1 2016.* Accessed at www.nielsen .com/us/en/insights/report/2016/the-total-audience-report-q1-2016 on June 23, 2022.

Nunez, K. (2020, June 9). *5 benefits of metta meditation and how to do it.* Accessed at www.healthline.com/health/metta-meditation on September 26, 2022.

Orme-Johnson, D. W., & Barnes, V. A. (2014). Effects of the transcendental meditation technique on trait anxiety: A meta-analysis of randomized controlled trials. *Journal of Alternative and Complementary Medicine, 20*(5), 330–341.

Ovans, A. (2015, April 28). *How emotional intelligence became a key leadership skill.* Accessed at https://hbr.org/2015/04/how-emotional-intelligence-became-a-key-leadership-skill on September 30, 2022.

Panskepp, J., & Biven, L. (2012). *The archaeology of mind: Neuroevolutionary origins of human emotion.* New York: Norton.

Pfeifer, E., & Wittmann, M. (2020). Waiting, thinking, and feeling: Variations in the perception of time during silence. *Frontiers in Psychology, 11*, 602.

Plowman, N., & Plowman, C. (2022). *Insight timer* [Mobile app]. Google Play Store. Accessed at https://play.google.com/store/apps/details?id=com.spotlightsix.zentimerlite2&hl=en_US&gl=US on September 30, 2022.

Przybylski, A., & Weinstein, N. (2013). Can you connect with me now? How the presence of mobile communication technology influences face-to-face conversation quality. *Journal of Social and Personal Relationships, 30*(3), 237–246.

Puddicombe, A., & Pierson, R. (2022). *Headspace: Mindful meditation* [Mobile app]. Google Play Store. Accessed at https://play.google.com/store/apps/details?id=com.getsomeheadspace.android&hl=en_US&gl=US on September 30, 2022.

Puderbaugh, M., & Emmady, P. D. (2022, May 8). *Neuroplasticity.* Accessed at www.ncbi.nlm.nih.gov/books/NBK557811 on September 30, 2022.

Raes, F. (2011). The effect of self-compassion on the development of depression symptoms in a non-clinical sample. *Mindfulness, 2*(1), 33–36.

Rainie, L., & Zickuhr, K. (2015, August 26). *Americans' views on mobile etiquette.* Accessed at www.pewresearch.org/internet/2015/08/26/americans-views-on-mobile-etiquette on June 23, 2022.

Reb, J., Sim, S., Chintakananda, K., & Bhave, D. P. (2015). Leading with mindfulness: Exploring the relation of mindfulness with leadership behaviors, styles, and development. In J. Reb & P. W. B. Atkins (Eds.), *Mindfulness in organizations: Foundations, research, and applications* (pp. 256–284). Cambridge, England: Cambridge University Press.

Ricard, M. (2010). *Why meditate: Working with thoughts and emotions*. Carlsbad, CA: Hay House.

Richtel, M. (2019, April 5). The latest in military strategy: Mindfulness. *The New York Times*. Accessed at www.nytimes.com/2019/04/05/health/military -mindfulness-training.html on September 26, 2022.

Rod, K. (2015). Observing the effects of mindfulness-based meditation on anxiety and depression in chronic pain patients. *Psychiatria Danubina*, *27* (Suppl 1), S209–S211.

Roeser, R. W., Schonert-Reichl, K. A., Jha, A., Cullen, M., Wallace, L., Wilensky, R., et al. (2013). Mindfulness training and reductions in teacher stress and burnout: Results from two randomized, waitlist-control field trials. *Journal of Educational Psychology*, *105*(3), 787–804.

Sbarra, D. A., Smith, H. L., & Mehl, M. R. (2013). When leaving your ex, love yourself: Observational ratings of self-compassion predict the course of emotional recovery following marital separation. *Psychological Science*, *23*(3), 261–269.

Schaufenbuel, K. (2015, December 28). *Why Google, Target, and General Mills are investing in mindfulness*. Accessed at https://hbr.org/2015/12/why-google -target-and-general-mills-are-investing-in-mindfulness on June 23, 2022.

Schonert-Reichl, K. A., & Lawlor, M. S. (2010). The effects of mindfulness-based program on pre- and early adolescents' well-being and social and emotional competence. *Mindfulness*, *1*(3) 137–151.

Schwartz, T. (2010, June). *The productivity paradox: How Sony Pictures gets more out of people by demanding less*. Accessed at https://hbr.org/2010/06/the -productivity-paradox-how-sony-pictures-gets-more-out-of-people-by -demanding-less on June 23, 2022.

Scott, D. A., Valley, B., & Simecka, B. A. (2017). Mental health concerns in the digital age. *International Journal of Mental Health and Addiction*, *15*(3), 604–613.

Scott, E. S. (2022, August 8). *What is stress? Your body's response to a situation that requires attention or action*. Accessed at www.verywellmind.com/stress-and -health-3145086 on September 26, 2022.

Scott, S. J. (2017, December 18). *What is mindful listening? With 7 activities for successful listening.* Accessed at www.developgoodhabits.com/mindful-listening on October 3, 2022.

Scruggs-Hussein, T. (2021, August 17). *A 12-minute meditation to set the tone for your leadership.* Accessed at www.mindful.org/a-12-minute-meditation-to-set-the-tone-for-your-leadership on June 23, 2022.

Seaver, M. (2020, October 1). *What mindfulness does to your brain: The science of neuroplasticity.* Accessed at www.realsimple.com/health/mind-mood/mindfulness-improves-brain-health-neuroplasticity on June 23, 2022.

Seppälä, E. M., Nitschke, J. B., Tudorascu, D. L., Hayes, A., Goldstein, M. R., Nguyen, D. T. H., et al. (2014). Breathing-based meditation decreases posttraumatic stress disorder symptoms in U. S. military veterans: A randomized controlled longitudinal study. *Journal of Traumatic Stress, 27*(4), 397–405.

Shafir, R. Z. (2000). *The zen of listening: Mindful communication in the age of distraction.* Wheaton, IL: Quest Books.

Shakespeare, W. (2016). *Hamlet, prince of Denmark.* B. Mowat & P. Werstine (Eds.). Accessed at https://folgerdigitaltexts.org/html/Ham.html#line-1.3.0 on October 14, 2022. (Original work published 1599)

Shapiro, S. L., Astin, J. A., Bishop, S. R., & Cordova, M. (2005). Mindfulness-based stress reduction for health care professionals: Results from a randomized trial. *International Journal of Stress Management, 12*(2), 164–176.

Shapiro, S. L., Brown, K. W., & Biegel, G. M. (2007). Teaching self-care to caregivers: Effects of mindfulness-based stress reduction on the mental health of therapists in training. *Training and Education in Professional Psychology, 1*(2), 105–115.

Shapiro, S. L., Carlson, L. E., Astin, J. A., & Freedman, B. S. (2006). Mechanisms of mindfulness. *Journal of Clinical Psychology, 62*(3), 373–386.

Siegel, D. J. (2007). *The mindful brain: Reflection and attunement in the cultivation of well-being.* New York: Norton.

Siegel, D. J. (2010). *Mindsight: The new science of personal transformation.* New York: Bantam Books.

Six Seconds. (2021, July 12). *Q: What's more important: EQ or mindfulness? A: They complement each other perfectly. When we bring our whole HEART and* [Image attached][Status update]. Facebook. Accessed at www.facebook.com/sixseconds/photos/a.10157378015432862/10158774692822862/?type=3 on October 3, 2022.

Smith, M. A., & Tew, A. (2012). *Calm* [Mobile app]. Google Play Store. Accessed at https://play.google.com/store/apps/details?id=com.calm.android&hl=en_US&gl=US on September 30, 2022.

Sofer, O. J. (2018, October 27). *Learning how to listen* [Blog post]. Accessed at www.orenjaysofer.com/blog/mindful-listening on October 3, 2022.

Sousa, D. A. (2011). *How the brain learns* (4th ed.). Thousand Oaks, CA: Corwin Press.

Spencer, B. (2013, February 10). *Mobile users can't leave their phones alone for six minutes and check it up to 150 times a day.* Accessed at www.dailymail.co.uk/news/article-2276752/Mobile-users-leave-phone-minutes-check-150-times-day.html on June 23, 2022.

Stahl, B. (2018, July 26). *Find balance during a moment of panic.* Accessed at www.mindful.org/find-balance-during-a-moment-of-panic on June 23, 2022.

Stanley, E. A., Schaldach, J. M., Kiyonaga, A., & Jha, A. P. (2011). Mindfulness-based mind fitness training: A case study of a high-stress predeployment military cohort. *Cognitive and Behavioral Practice, 18*(4), 566–576.

Stedham, Y., & Skaar, T. B. (2019). Mindfulness, trust, and leader effectiveness: A conceptual framework. *Frontiers in Psychology, 10*, 1588.

Steiner, E. D., Doan, S., Woo, A., Gittens, A. D., Lawrence, R. A., Berdie, L., et al. (2022). *Restoring teacher and principal well-being is an essential step for rebuilding schools: Findings from the State of the American Teacher and State of the American Principal surveys.* Accessed at www.rand.org/pubs/research_reports/RRA1108-4.html on September 30, 2022.

Stibich, M. (2020, April 24). *How to sit when learning meditation.* Accessed at www.verywellmind.com/how-to-sit-when-learning-to-meditate-2224121 on October 3, 2022.

Suzuki, S. (2020). *Zen mind, beginner's mind* (50th anniversary ed.). Boulder, CO: Shambhala.

Tacón, A. M., McComb, J., Caldera, Y., & Randolph, P. (2003). Mindfulness meditation anxiety reduction, and heart disease: A pilot study. *Family & Community Health*, *26*(1), 25–33.

Tan, C. M. (2012). *Search inside yourself: The unexpected path to achieving success, happiness (and world peace)*. New York: HarperOne.

Tenney, M. (2022). *What is mindful leadership? Why is it essential for success?* Accessed at https://themindfulnessedge.com/what-is-mindful-leadership on June 23, 2022.

Toepfer, S. M., Cichy, K., & Peters, P. (2012). Letters of gratitude: Further evidence for author benefits. *Journal of Happiness Studies*, *13*(1), 187–201.

Tsafou, K.-E., De Ridder, D. T., van Ee, R., & Lacroix, J. P. (2016). Mindfulness and satisfaction in physical activity: A cross-sectional study in the Dutch population. *Journal of Health Psychology*, *21*(9), 1817–1827.

UCLA Mindful Awareness Research Center. (2022). *UCLA mindful* [Mobile app]. Google Play Store. Accessed at https://play.google.com/store/apps/details?id=org.uclahealth.marc&hl=en_US&gl=US on September 30, 2022.

University of British Columbia. (2018, May 3). *Mindfulness at work: Study first to uncover positive benefits for teams*. Accessed at www.sciencedaily.com/releases/2018/05/180503142625.htm on September 7, 2022.

University of Virginia School of Medicine Mindfulness Center. (n.d.). *Mindful writing*. Accessed at https://med.virginia.edu/mindfulness-center/continue-your-practice/mindful-writing on September 26, 2022.

Vengoechea, X. (2021). *Listen like you mean it: Reclaiming the lost art of true connection*. New York: Penguin.

Wallace Foundation. (2013, January). *The school principal as leader: Guiding schools to better teaching and learning*. Accessed at www.wallacefoundation.org/knowledge-center/pages/the-school-principal-as-leader-guiding-schools-to-better-teaching-and-learning.aspx on June 23, 2022.

Weeks, H. (2010). *Failure to communicate: How conversations go wrong and what you can do to right them*. Boston: Harvard Business Press.

Wells, C. M. (2015). *Conceptualizing mindful leadership in schools: How the practice of mindfulness informs the practice of leading*. Accessed at https://files.eric.ed.gov/fulltext/EJ1105711.pdf on June 23, 2022.

Weng, H. Y., Fox, A. S., Shackman, A. J., Stodola, D. E., Caldwell, J. Z. K., Olson, M. C., et al. (2013). Compassion training alters altruism and responses to suffering. *Psychological Science, 24*(7), 1171–1180.

Whitfield, T., Barnhofer, T., Acabchuk, R., Cohen, A., Lee, M., Schlosser, M., et al. (2022). The effect of mindfulness-based programs on cognitive function in adults: A systematic review and meta-analysis. *Neuropsychology Review, 32*(3), 677–702.

Williams, M., & Penman, D. (2011). *Mindfulness: An eight-week plan for finding peace in a frantic world.* Emmaus, PA: Rodale Books.

Wilson, J. (2014). *Mindful America: The mutual transformation of Buddhist meditation and American culture.* New York: Oxford University Press.

Winning, A. P., & Boag, S. (2015). Does brief mindfulness training increase empathy? The role of personality. *Personality and Individual Differences, 86,* 492–498.

Wolf, C., & Serpa, J. G. (2015). *A clinician's guide to teaching mindfulness: The comprehensive session-by-session program for mental health professionals and health care providers.* Oakland, CA: New Harbinger.

Yang, C.-H., & Conroy, D. E. (2018). Momentary negative affect is lower during mindful movement than while sitting: An experience sampling study. *Psychology of Sport and Exercise, 37,* 109–116.

Yates, A. (2022, July 6). *How the Insight Timer app can improve your well-being.* Accessed at www.makeuseof.com/deep-dive-into-insight-timer-meditation-app on October 3, 2022.

Yuko, E. (2020, August 17). *Why intentional silence may be the form of meditation that actually works for you.* Accessed at https://realsimple.com/health/mind-mood/intermittent-silence on September 30, 2022.

Index

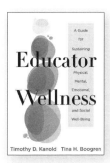

Educator Wellness
Timothy D. Kanold and Tina H. Boogren

How do we bring our best selves to our students and colleagues each day? Designed as a reflective journal and guidebook, _Educator Wellness_ will take you on a deep exploration where you will uncover profound answers that ring true for you.
BKG053

Coaching for Educator Wellness
Tina H. Boogren

Acquire evergreen coaching strategies alongside fresh new solutions for differentiating support for new and veteran teachers, addressing teacher self-care, and more. You'll turn to this resource again and again as you continue to improve your craft and help teachers find their own greatness.
BKF989

Beyond Self-Care
Gail Markin

Explore the importance of well-being at individual, group, and system levels, as well as the role of leadership in supporting school cultures of well-being. Using research-based practices and excerpts of conversations from working educators, Markin delivers a guidebook to healthier, more passionate schools.
BKG079

Cultivating Mindfulness in the Classroom
Jeanie M. Iberlin

Discover practical tools that align to the five key categories of mindfulness benefits—stress reduction, attention, emotional control, positive self-concept, and positive interactions—and explore a step-by-step process for establishing a formal school or classroom mindfulness program.
BKL035

MARZANO Resources

Visit MarzanoResources.com or call 888.849.0851 to order.

Professional Development
Designed for Success

Empower your staff to tap into their full potential as educators. As an all-inclusive research-into-practice resource center, we are committed to helping your school or district become highly effective at preparing every student for his or her future.

Choose from our wide range of customized professional development opportunities for teachers, administrators, and district leaders. Each session offers hands-on support, personalized answers, and accessible strategies that can be put into practice immediately.

Bring Marzano Resources experts to your school for results-oriented training on:

- ▶ Assessment & Grading
- ▶ Curriculum
- ▶ Instruction
- ▶ School Leadership

- ▶ Teacher Effectiveness
- ▶ Student Engagement
- ▶ Vocabulary
- ▶ Competency-Based Education

LEARN MORE at MarzanoResources.com/PD